Next Dimension Access to the Court of Supplications

Understanding

Supplications, Requisitions, & Acquisitions

By

Dr. Ron M. Horner

Next Dimension Access to the Court of Supplications

Understanding
Supplications, Requisitions, & Acquisitions

By

Dr. Ron M. Horner

LifeSpring Publishing
PO Box 5847
Pinehurst, North Carolina 28374 USA
www.RonHorner.com

Next Dimension Access to the Court of Supplications

Understanding Supplications, Requisitions & Acquisitions

Copyright © 2024 Dr. Ron M. Horner

Scripture is taken from the New King James Version®. Copyright © 1982 by Thomas Nelson. Used with permission. All rights reserved. (Unless otherwise noted.)

Scripture quotations are taken from the Amplified® Bible (AMP), Copyright © 1954, 1958, 1962, 1964, 1965, 1987 by The Lockman Foundation.

Scripture marked (THE MIRROR) is taken from The Mirror Study Bible by Francois du Toit. Copyright © 2021 All Rights Reserved. Used by permission of The Author.

All rights reserved. This book is protected by the copyright laws of the United States of America. This book may not be copied or reprinted for commercial gain or profit. The use of short quotations or occasional page copying for personal, or group study is permitted and encouraged. Permission will be granted upon request.

Requests for bulk sales discounts, editorial permissions, or other information should be addressed to:

LifeSpring Publishing
PO Box 5847
Pinehurst, NC 28374 USA

Additional copies available at: www.ronhorner.com

ISBN 13 TP: 978-1-953684-56-1
ISBN 13 eBook: 978-1-953684-57-8

Cover Design by Darian Horner Design
(www.darianhorner.com)
Image: 123rf.com #224925361

First Edition: June 2024

10 9 8 7 6 5 4 3 2 1 0

Printed in the United States of America

Table of Contents

Acknowledgments i
Foreword iii
Characters Mentioned vii
Preface ix
Chapter 1 Understanding the Court
  of Supplications & Acquisitions 1
Chapter 2 Your Prayers Are Not a Secret from Heaven .. 7
Chapter 3 Dealing with Petitions on Appeal 15
Chapter 4 Liens on Supplications 35
Chapter 5 Access the Court Through Jesus 45
Chapter 6 Working Through Your Petitions 49
Chapter 7 It's About Intimacy 57
Chapter 8 Your Personal Court
  of Supplications & Acquisitions 67
Chapter 9 Accessing Ease for Your Soul 71
Chapter 10 Accessing Your Mountain of Intimacy 79
Chapter 11 Run With It 87
Chapter 12 Future Adjudication 99
Chapter 13 Basic Rules for Supplications 105
Chapter 14 Naming the Requisition 113

Chapter 15 Acquisitions 119

Chapter 16 What are you saying? 123

Chapter 17 A Daily Routine? 129

Chapter 18 Greater Measure 133

Chapter 19 Becoming a Friend 141

Chapter 20 Epilogue 145

Appendix 149

Resources for Scripture Research 151

Resources from LifeSpring International Ministries .. 153

Description 157

About the Author 159

Other Books by Dr. Ron M. Horner 161

Acknowledgments

Books never appear out of thin air. They come with the assistance, support, and prayers of a team of people. The team at LifeSpring that helped with this book includes teams of intercessors who access Heaven on our behalf, and support staff; including my Executive Assistant, Stephanie Stanfill; Wendy Selvig, editor; and Darian Horner, who handles formatting and design of the book. David Porter also assisted in the engagements with Heaven. These are just a few who assist us. We also have the privilege of working with a team of men and women in white and a host of angels who aid us in a myriad of ways. To all, I say thank you.

Foreword

For many years, I have been on a quest seeking God for His revelation regarding His kingdom. For several decades as a prophetic apostle, senior pastor, and itinerant minister, I always knew that there was more to learn about God and his Kingdom. I would often say to the congregation, "We live and operate in dual dimensions at the same time." I did not realize at the time the depth of how true that statement was. Since that time, I have come to know that not only do we live in dual dimensions—multiple dimensions are available to us as believers.

It was in the fall of 2020. as I was looking for further knowledge and revelation of God, that I came across a series of teachings regarding the Courts of Heaven. It was also during that time that I discovered the Courts of Heaven teaching by Dr. Ron Horner. That began my journey in the Courts of Heaven and with Dr. Ron. As time passed, I became very involved with LifeSpring International Ministries. I became a part of the Facilitator Training Program Class of 2021. I became involved as a Junior Advocate, helping people to navigate through the Courts of Heaven. I was offered a position with the ministry in their accounting department, which I presently hold.

In addition, once relocating to Pinehurst, NC, Heaven established Sandhills Ecclesia where I serve as lead apostle alongside Dr Ron and Adina Horner. It has been my honor to watch, listen, and learn how to navigate in the Courts of Heaven. To experience what Heaven is doing now with the sons of God at times is excitedly overwhelming because of the magnitude that the revelations from Heaven are releasing to the sons. My life has been impacted and empowered. My understanding, my relationship with the Father, with Jesus, and Holy Spirit and all the hosts of Heaven have kept me in awe and gratefulness that the Father has ordained my steps in this way.

Once again Heaven has used Dr. Ron Horner to pin another revelation that I believe will accelerate the body of Christ to greater sonship maturity. The book of Hebrews 12:31 speaks of "a more excellent way." The book that you hold in your hand and that you are about to read will be a major tool for getting your prayers answered and changing the way that you do intercession.

If there ever was a time that the sons of God and the world needed to see the Kingdom of God come to Earth as it is in Heaven, now is the time. The revelation in this book would teach you, empower you, and equip you to utilize the Court of Supplication and Acquisitions and its protocols to receive answers to prayer. I am humbled and honored to be asked to write the Foreword for this book.

Words cannot adequately express my heartfelt and deep love and appreciation for this highly anointed, chosen son of God and General, Dr. Ron Horner.

David Nathan Porter III
Prophetic Apostle

Characters Mentioned

Adina – Dr. Ron Horner's beautiful wife, co-founder, and Chief Financial Officer of LifeSpring

Angela – a woman in white who assists Gloria in legal matters.

David Porter– serves as Lead Apostle of Sandhills Ecclesia as well as our chief accountant.

Ezekiel – the Chief Angel over LifeSpring International Ministries, Inc.

George – a man in white who serves as the Financial Advisor for LifeSpring

Gloria – a woman in white who serves as our Legal Counsel in the LifeSpring complex.

Jen Jones – serves as the director of our AfterCare program.

Jonathan – a man in white who assists us in the Library of Revelation. He was the son of King Saul.

Kevin Boehmer – serves as the Director of CourtsNet and the FTP program.

Jeremy Friedman – is the Director of Heaven Down Business.

Jonathan – a man in white who assists us in the Library of Revelation. He was the son of King Saul.

Magistrate – the magistrate in the Court of Supplications and Acquisitions.

Malcolm – a man in white who tutors us in the things of Heaven.

Samuel – A man in white who assists us in the Library of Revelation

Stephanie Stanfill – serves as Dr. Ron's Executive Assistant.

Wisdom – the entity Wisdom, sometimes referred to as Lady Wisdom.

———·———

Preface

In over 50 years of ministry, I have seen marvelous answers to prayer, and I have experienced many as yet unanswered prayers. I do not blame Heaven for the unanswered ones. Somewhere along the way, I failed to follow the proper protocol, came out of agreement, or asked for the wrong reason. All are reasons (among many others) that we may experience unanswered prayers.

The basic premise of the Courts of Heaven prayer paradigm is:

---

*If you have a prayer
that has not been answered,
there is a legal reason.
Once the legal reason is taken care of,
the answer can come.*

It is simple, and it makes sense. We are told in Matthew 6 that if we have unforgiveness in our hearts, it can hinder things. In James, we learn that if we ask with the wrong motivation, our prayer will not be heard.

I do not know about you, but if I am going to go to the effort to pray, I may as well do it properly and meet the conditions. The conditions are not demanding, but they must be met. We will even experience the mercy of the Father to work with us through and in spite of mistakes we might make along the way.

In all my years of ministry, I do not ever recall hearing a teaching on supplication. That has its pluses and its minuses. Perhaps I never heard teaching on it because others never really understood it either. The advantage I had when I started with the engagement at the end of 2023 was that I did not have a lot of wrong understandings to deal with. I simply did not have a lot of understanding, period.

The subtitle of this book is:

*"Understanding Supplications,
Requisitions & Acquisitions."*

The Courts of Heaven is just one of the three paradigms of prayer taught by Jesus: the son to Father paradigm, the friend-to-friend (both found in Luke 11), and the Courts of Heaven paradigm found in Luke 18. It is from this paradigm that this book is written. Like all courts (both in Heaven and on Earth), certain protocols exist for operation within a particular court that must be followed. I never want to be ejected from a heavenly court because I violated the protocol of that court, nor do you.

Protocols are like guardrails on a highway. They keep you within the boundaries, so you do not run off into the ditch. They are helpful guides to keep you safe. Always treat protocols as safety mechanisms and not barriers to something. If I will honor the protocols of a particular court, I can experience the benefits of the purpose of that court. The principle is:

---
*What I honor,
I can have the benefit of.*

I have never been a proponent of simply bee-bopping up to a court and acting like I owned it. Privilege may give me access, but honor will keep me in it and because I honor a court, I will ask permission, not merely assume things about that court. It has been proven over and over that the Father wants to give good gifts to His children.[1] I simply need to follow the rules.

The pattern of Heaven concerning the Court of Supplications and Acquisitions is as follows:

Petition+Legal Precedent (applicable scripture) creates a supplication. The supplication then becomes a requisition in order to result in an acquisition (of the thing desired). In this book on supplications and petitions we will discover that many prayers have yet to be answered simply because we omitted a detail or two. As you read these engagements, we will learn some of these omissions and how to remedy them.

---
[1] Matthew 7:11

In Daniel 9, we read that Daniel made request to God by prayer and supplication that ended in the freedom of the Children of Israel from captivity by the Babylonians. His prayer and supplication had national implications.

Solomon offered up prayer and supplication in 1 Kings 8 that resulted in blessing upon the nation.

In Acts 1, the disciples met in the upper room and, with one accord in prayer and supplication, made requests of the Lord. Their petitions were granted and on the Day of Pentecost, the Heavens overflowed with the acquisition of the plan of God for that special day in history. That story is one of the powers of corporate prayer and supplication.

If one can put a thousand to flight and two can put ten thousand to flight, what about one hundred saints praying in one accord? What would happen? Dare we find out?

Later, Paul includes the act of prayer with prayer and supplication as one of the tools in our spiritual tool kit. It is a part of our armor. He expanded it to include doing it in the spirit or in our prayer language, not just in our native language.

Our prayer language should be our native language.

The best way to turn a petition into a supplication is to be Heaven down and spirit forward. A typical definition of a supplication is an earnest prayer. However, Heaven's definition seems to be an earnest request made with legal precedent (supporting scriptures) to back the request.

The very best way to be spirit forward is to pray in your prayer language. Sometimes, you will find yourself praying in tongues while, at the same time, understanding what you are praying for. At times, you may be developing a petition that will result in a supplication when you add scriptures relevant to the felt need and present those before the Court of Supplications and Acquisitions. Remember, supplications are to end up with acquisitions.

In Philippians 4:6, we are instructed to make prayer and supplication coupled *with* thanksgiving to make our requests known to God. Thanks is what you give when you have received something. As we make supplication before the Lord, we should see it as already done, and because it is done, we can give thanks to the supplier of the need. Paul told us in Philippians 4:19 that God will supply all your needs according to His riches—not according to our riches, but according to *His* riches in Glory. He will make replete everything the need requires so that you are amply supplied.

In this simple book, I will present this revelation as we received it in a series of engagements with Heaven, men, and women in white, angels, Holy Spirit, the Seven Spirits of God, and within Personal Advocacy Sessions with clients. Heaven will often teach us as we are conducting sessions. It is our OJT (On the Job Training). You will experience that as well.

If you were to ask any fellow believer in Jesus if they would like to see *all* their supplications answered, they would invariably tell you, 'Yes.'

If you were to ask them if they were willing to follow the rules to see that happen, hopefully, they would answer yes to that as well.

As we were to learn, there are some basic requirements with some basic rules that must be followed, but we will experience great grace as we go through this process and see answers to our prayers met in an unprecedented manner…simply by following the rules.

Basic Rules for Supplications

1. Make your request in faith (Hebrews 11:6)
2. Make your request according to the will of God (Is it in alignment with the Word of God?) (James 4:3, 1 John 5:21-22, Philippians 1:6)
3. Have scriptural precedent to support your petition.
4. If you come into agreement, do not come out of agreement. (Matthew 18:19) See it through to the full manifestation.
5. Give thanks for the "already done" supplication because it IS already done! (Proverbs 3:5-6) speaks to the posture of the heart. Be careful what you say—even the position of your heart. There must be NO place where the supplication cannot be granted. That is why it must be based on the Word of God.
6. Understand the purpose (Proverbs 8:21 That I may cause those who love me to inherit wealth, That I may fill their treasuries. **God wants you**

to be blessed. (Proverbs 10:22, Psalm 68:19, Deuteronomy 28:1-2, John 15:7)
7. Declare your receipt of the thing needed or desired aloud. (Mark 11:24)

From what we understand, the information we are sharing was first released to some other ministries, but for some reason, they were unwilling to receive and disseminate it. A little over two years ago a treasure chest was delivered to me in an engagement with Heaven. It was locked, and the angel said it contained revelation that was supposed to have been released several years ago, but the recipient(s) refused to embrace it and therefore it was never released. Because it was never released, it was re-released to us. I was instructed to keep it until the appointed time. The time is now. We are glad for the opportunity to make this openly available to the Body of Christ. We want to be responsible stewards of this revelation and stewards of the practice of it.

Heaven had this to say specifically about it now:

This book was here before the foundation of the world. It was placed in this library when Ron accepted the commission to write. Others were given the opportunity and they rejected it.

The opportunity to step into this portal was given many times before, but many were fearful of what men would say and rejected the revelation out of fear—the fear of man. But because you have sought the Lord, this purpose, the face of the Father, His will, and His heart, you have been given access.

You've not just been given access, but you are being taught how to navigate and how to matriculate, not just from this place, not just from this court, but from other courts that have not been accessed before. The Father desires to give you the Kingdom. He has sought others, and you have been one who has humbly submitted, obeyed, and answered the call.

Then Gloria said something very funny. She said, "Hold onto your wigs. You are in for a ride!"

Now, call your spirit forward, ask your soul to take a seat of rest and be a bridge, not a gatekeeper, concerning the revelation you are about to receive. If while reading this book you must stop and do something else, simply call your spirit forward each time you pick up the book to start reading it again. It will help you be in the right framework for the revelation coming forth.

Also, as you read, Heaven will download information to you about prayers you have prayed that need to be put in supplication form so the answers can come from Heaven. You might want to have a notebook or notepad handy to jot down things that will come to mind so you can more thoroughly take care of them later. This is going to be an enriching time for you as together we explore the Court of Supplications and Acquisitions. Let's have fun together!

. . . .

Ending Note

As David and I checked in at the Library of Revelation (in Heaven) to see if anything else needed to be added to this book, Samuel met us and began, "You do realize that this book is about principles and revelations. They are one and the same. There is nothing more to put in the book, but it is imperative that those who read this revelation embrace it and use the principles that are within. Exercise the principles like you would use an instruction manual.

"Advise the readers not to move through the book quickly, but to prayerfully digest and receive each revelation, each process, each step. Each step is like a building block, like a puzzle, and it will unfold the revelation. The revelations are dimensional as well.

"They need to understand that in the Court of Supplications, the enemy has no access. It is exclusively for the sons. Through the sons the Kingdom of Heaven will manifest in the earth. They are the catalyst for the multiplication of this revelation, as in other revelations. But this revelation is special because **it changes the trajectory of intercession as you have known in your earth realm**."

This revelation puts you at the head of the class. It puts you at the beginning of the wave. Revelations come—some catch it in the beginning, some will catch it in the middle, and some will catch it in the end. You are leading this out. You are at the head of the wave of this revelation. There is another phase, but at this time, I was instructed only to release this portion of it.

This book is to lead and guide the sons into a greater understanding, a greater awareness, and a greater embrace of their sonship and how to be used in the hand of the Father. With this revelation, it would be like swords piercing the darkness, bringing deliverance, and setting captives free. As people come into this revelation like a sword might chop through thick chains, so this revelation will break bondages. This is the reason that Jesus came to destroy the works of darkness. This revelation will be used in that manner.

———·———

Chapter 1
Understanding the Court of Supplications & Acquisitions

At the end of 2023, my Executive Assistant Stephanie and I were introduced to a new court: the Court of Supplications and Acquisitions. It is one of the many courts within the Courts of Heaven. The Courts of Heaven prayer paradigm is a prayer paradigm that has just in the last few years been unveiled in the Body of Christ. I have been fortunate to have been one of the early pioneers regarding the Courts of Heaven and have watched it mature and expand on the earth. We are still learning about various courts and their protocols. This engagement would continue to unfold in the coming months, resulting in the book you are reading today.

That engagement was primarily just an introduction. However, we had been told by Gloria, a woman in white who serves as the legal advisor for our ministry, that this was an earned place. We had been granted access due to proper stewardship in other areas of the Courts of Heaven.

Some may be taken aback by that seeming restriction on one of the Courts of Heaven, but it is perfectly in line with what Joshua, the High Priest, was told by the Lord in Zechariah 3:7:

> *Thus says the LORD of hosts: 'If you will walk in My ways, and if you will keep My command, then you shall also judge My house, and likewise have charge of My courts; I will give you places to walk among these who stand here.'*

The Christian walk is built around stewardship which that passage outlines. Because we had been faithful stewards of other courts and the protocols of those courts, we had been granted access to this court. We were grateful.

From this courtroom, we could see other courts as if you could access other courts (even celestial ones) from this courtroom. They were in other dimensions but were quickly accessible from this courtroom.

We watched as Gloria spoke to the judge and then to Ezekiel, the Chief Angel over LifeSpring, who presented evidence and scrolls to the judge; then, having heard the instructions, he turned and left. At that point, Henry, a man in white whom we had assisted in his transition to Heaven some years before and who now assisted Gloria, came, and stood with her. The Court of Times and Seasons then came into action. We saw a wheel turning and a clock turning as well. A tapestry was rolled out in front of us. Also, an interrogatory[2] was presented to us.

We found ourselves standing on the beautiful tapestry that we knew represented many nations and represented what LifeSpring was doing with people of many nations. As we watched, more details of the courtroom came into view as if it were morphing from the original scene of one judge behind the judge's bench to a long table with a panel of judges seated behind it. The Spirit of Wisdom was standing nearby. A council of three was also seated in another location that included the Spirit of Knowledge, the Spirit of Understanding, and the Spirit of the Reverential Fear of the Lord. A banner flanked the entire ceiling.

Gloria, who had been standing before the judge, turned and came behind the knee wall and stood in front of us. Speaking to us, she said, "This is your new position of authority. This is where you will state your cases. The enemy is not welcome here."

Unlike some courts where the accuser might be present, as we read in Job 1 and 2, he was not welcome in this courtroom, not even through what we would call a video feed.

Gloria continued with instructions to us. She said, "Be careful or be aware that out of the abundance of the heart, the mouth speaks."

---

[2] In court settings, an interrogatory is a question or series of questions that must be answered by the opposing part in a court case.

Supplication is the act of asking for something earnestly.

Jeremiah 36:7:

It may be that they will present their supplication before the LORD, and everyone will turn from his evil way. For great is the anger and the fury that the LORD has pronounced against this people.

We can define supplication as a form of prayer, a call for help from God. The term bears a **spirit of reverence,** which is why we noted the Spirit of The Reverential Fear of the Lord was one of the counsel seated off to the right.

Not wanting to dishonor the court, we asked Gloria, "How do we navigate this properly? We want to honor the court and we are grateful and thankful to the king for allowing us to have access to this court and be a part of this court. Is there a docket that we are to follow?"

Gloria replied, "I will carry the docket, and you are to mind your mouth because out of the abundance of the heart, the mouth speaks."

Stephanie responded, "Well, I know that I must be careful with my heart. Please help us to understand the docket and the protocol to walk through this."

Gloria continued, "The court knows you're willing to do it, which is why you're here (pointing to the other side of this knee wall, the side where the audience sits.)."

I asked what we were to witness that day, and Gloria replied, "The establishment of your position in this place.

There is no delay here. In what you would consider delay. There is no delay in this position."

"Can we step ahead into the future and adjudicate here?" I asked,

Gloria replied, "I thought you would never ask. It is my specialty."

I responded that we were willing. We were reminded of a prior engagement when the angel Neopol took us to the future and then brought us back.

Gloria stated, "That was the beginning."

We will discuss this in a future engagement. Look for it!

Chapter 2

Your Prayers Are Not a Secret from Heaven

As that engagement ended, a short time later we were engaging with Heaven again and found ourselves with Gloria. She seemed serious and stated, "This is serious stuff."

This time, we went down the hall in this complex and to the left to a courtroom. There was a magistrate.[3]

As we entered the courtroom, the magistrate had Stephanie stand behind him as if to watch the proceedings from his viewpoint. She looked on the magistrate's bench and saw records of supplications (which are prayers made by petition).

---

[3] "A magistrate typically handles minor cases and pretrial matters, often without a jury. A judge presides over more serious cases, conducts trials with or without a jury, and has broader legal authority. Both uphold justice but with varying scopes and responsibilities." *OpenAI*. (2024) ChatGPT (April 16 3.5) https://chat.openai.com/chat

The Magistrate remarked that we could make petitions in this Court. "This is a Court of Supplications," he explained.

As Stephanie looked around, she saw Gloria sitting at the front of the courtroom in the first chair. Then, the Magistrate showed her a ledger.

The Magistrate explained, "These are supplications, and they are backed by the word. They are different from decrees because you can decree something without having a biblical foundation for it. Supplications have scripture to support it and to provide legal precedence."

Explaining to Stephanie how I understood a supplication worked, I said, "For example, if you were requesting provision, you could base it on Philippians 4:19:

And my God shall supply all your need according to His riches in glory by Christ Jesus."

The magistrate smiled and nodded as I asked him if my surmising was correct.

The Magistrate explained, "That's correct. There is also a Court of Decrees, but that is a different court with a different magistrate. Here, you can bring your supplication *backed by the word."*

He showed Stephanie pages of supplications containing a short, simple paragraph of a prayer with the Biblical reference underneath it done in a ledger style. In the middle of the page, there was a line drawn down the center of it and to the right were the court's rulings.

She noticed one that was not yet ruled upon and asked for an explanation.

Heaven knows ahead of time who is coming to bring supplications.

The Magistrate explained, "Heaven knows ahead of time who is coming to bring these supplications. The person for this ruling has not brought it before the court yet. However, Heaven already knows what you are going to say before you say it and what you are going to pray before you pray it. Therefore, it is already written; it just needs a ruling."[4]

In the prior engagement, Psalm 19:14 was written above and behind the judge's bench:

Let the words in my mouth and the meditation of my heart be acceptable or pleasing in your sight, my strength, and my redeemer.

The Magistrate explained, "The focus is that you watch what you say. What you say is what you will end up with."

Stephanie noted, "This will kind of make people get in the word a little bit more."

The Magistrate replied, "That's the idea."

---

[4] Matthew 6:8, Therefore do not be like them. For your Father knows the things you have need of before you ask Him.

If you have a need, find out what scripture you can use as backing for that need.

The Magistrate explained, "There are not a lot of people that gain this access. Not everybody comes this direction (to this court)."

Stephanie remarked, "I saw this scene going backward, as if Heaven rewound this scene of me and Gloria. We were walking backward, going out before we came in. I am getting the knowing that the way into this court is intimacy with the Father and Jesus. Not everybody comes this direction, through intimacy and through seeking out the Word."

I asked, "Is this a stewardship-based court?"

The Magistrate replied, "Correct."

I said, "From what I recall from the previous engagement, we got here because we had done court work faithfully in other courts."

Stephanie was reminded that she had been praying for her daughters and speaking to the Magistrate; she said, "For example, the prayer that I've had on my heart about my children where I have said that my children are my inheritance…"

The Magistrate turned the page in the ledger and showed her the page with that petition. A ruling on it already existed—a righteous judgment on her behalf for that supplication.

I was reminded that in the prior engagement, Gloria would have the docket for what needed to be dealt with in this court. I asked if we needed to present anything before the judge. Gloria then handed the docket to Stephanie to hand to the Magistrate. Even before he opened it, he said, "You know that you're in good standing."

Stephanie replied, "That's good to know, Magistrate." And he opened the docket. On the ledger was a line item of every supplication. Not every supplication had a scripture beside it, but most of them did. We realized we had some petitions we needed to add scriptures to. When you add scripture to a petition, you are presenting a legal precedence for that petition to be answered.

Seeking an example, it came to mind that as part of my daily governing for LifeSpring and Heaven Down Business where I state that I will not permit disunity and disharmony, I needed to add scriptures to support this prayer. Then, the petition would become a legal case as a supplication.

I then began to recite a scripture I had read that morning from 1 Corinthians 1:10, which states,

> *Friends, because we are surnamed and identified in the name of our master Jesus Christ, I urge you to speak with one voice. We share the same source as our reference. The idea of division is an illusion, we are a perfect match, accurately joined in the same thought and communicating the same result. (MIRROR)*

As I read the passage, Stephanie watched it appear on the page. I then saw a second scripture that states, "How can two walk together unless they are agreed (Amos 3:3).

A third scripture came to mind from Matthew 18:19:

If any two of you agree as touching anything that they would ask, it would be done by Father, which is in Heaven.

We asked the Magistrate if we could have this prayer as a supplication. In beautiful calligraphy script, we saw him write "Granted."

Stephanie noted, "When you were talking, Ron, I saw Jesus on the back row because there are rows of seats in this court. I saw him on the back left-hand side, and we had a mental conversation with one another."

Jesus said, "You're here because of your connection and your intimacy—our relationship."

When the Magistrate wrote "Granted," Jesus said, "I second that!"

We asked if other prayers needed scripture, and the Magistrate suggested, "Let's talk about sickness among the brethren."

3 John 2 came to mind, which states, "I wish above all things that you may prosper and be in health even as your soul prospers."

The Magistrate stated, "It has to be submitted as a supplication with that scripture."

Stephanie asked, "What would this supplication be?"

I replied, "That wholeness would be the children's bread for those that are associated with LifeSpring. And of course, we have a scripture about the children's bread" (Mark 7:26-29).

Stephanie said to the Magistrate, "How about adding 'by his stripes we are healed.'" (1 Peter 2:24).

The Magistrate exclaimed, "Granted."

Stephanie remarked how much she liked this court and got the impression that the Magistrate had been waiting for us and was very happy that we came.

We could see Ezekiel standing off to the left. He said, "My role is to implement these matters of the court."

Stephanie asked if we needed to call upon him and he explained that the Magistrate would call upon him when the petitions for that time were done.

Our next instruction was to build out a framework of supplications from each of the heads of the various departments of the ministry.

Stephanie remarked, "So—Jen for AfterCare, David for Sandhills Ecclesia, Jeremy for Heaven Down Business, Adina for Adina's Melodies, Kevin for CourtsNet and the FTP, and the others."

We put in these supplications for those coming up underneath my leadership.

I requested that each would be filled with Wisdom, Understanding and compassion based on Proverbs 1:2-7:

> *² To know wisdom and instruction, to perceive the words of understanding,*
>
> *³ To receive the instruction of wisdom, justice, judgment, and equity;*
>
> *⁴ To give prudence to the simple, to the young man knowledge and discretion—*
>
> *⁵ A wise man will hear and increase learning, and a man of understanding will attain wise counsel,*
>
> *⁶ To understand a proverb and an enigma, the words of the wise and their riddles.*
>
> *⁷ The fear of the LORD is the beginning of knowledge, but fools despise wisdom and instruction.*

We could see the ledger filled with supplications that had been answered.

——— · ———

Chapter 3

Dealing with Petitions on Appeal

The Magistrate then turned to the back of the ledger, and we saw the word "appeal."

He explained, "Some of these are on appeal."

Stephanie asked, "What does that mean? How do you mean they are on appeal?"

He replied, "The enemy has appealed some of them."

Stephanie could see that the appeal was based on what the accuser kept saying regarding "the truth of the matter."

I remarked, "For instance—"

The Magistrate asked, "What is the substance of things hoped for?"

Stephanie replied, "Faith."

The Magistrate explained, "There are some areas where the enemy knows that there's a lack of faith regarding certain matters which has caused an appeal."

Stephanie asked, "Is there a specific example?"

He asked if she believed she was healed.

She replied, "I have been fighting for that. Is that my lack of faith? Can you give me another example?"

He responded, "Agreements."

Stephanie saw the difference between what one person thinks should happen and what others think should happen regarding how we do things.

Stephanie stated, "But Magistrate, we can't control what other people's thoughts are."

He replied, "No, but you can forgive."

Stephanie responded, "Okay. We do forgive them for not fully agreeing with a matter."

She continued, "It seems like it would be difficult to manage, especially as we grow regarding many people's thought processes about matters."

The Magistrate replied, "It causes an appeal, nonetheless."

The scripture came up about *how can any walk together unless they agree* (Amos 3:3).

Stephanie asked, "When we meet with Gloria, we can just ask if there are any appeals against supplications?"

"Yes, you can," he replied.

I remarked, "Okay. For those who do not agree, we do forgive, bless, and release them for operating contrary to how we operate and not agreeing with our standards."

Stephanie asked, "May we request that this appeal be overturned by this court as supplication of unity with the scriptures that were spoken of before that were specifically about agreement?" *Where two or more agree upon a thing...* (Matthew 18:19). We wanted that scripture added to the supplication.

In response she saw the word *appeal* and he put a red X across it.

I asked, "At this point, does it go back to the regular listing on the ledger?"

The reply was, "Yes, it goes back over on the ledger side."

Reasons for Appeals

What are some other reasons the enemy might use to appeal a supplication? You have created a petition, you have added appropriate scriptures to provide legal precedent, you are standing in faith for that need, yet it the supplication has been appealed.

The enemy can know or at least presume that he can disqualify a supplication for any number of reasons. Here are some of the ones we have uncovered at this point.

Lack of Agreement

One of those reasons is a lack of agreement when agreement is required for a particular supplication. We will discuss an example of that in a short while.

Paul wrote in Colossians 1:15-17:

> *¹⁵ He (Jesus) is the image of the invisible God, the firstborn over all creation. ¹⁶ For by Him all things were created that are in heaven and that are on earth, visible and invisible, whether thrones or dominions or principalities or powers. All things were created through Him and for Him. ¹⁷ And He is before all things, and in Him all things consist.*

'All things' includes the provision for needs that you are not aware of the existence of that are waiting for this time to appear. You may have a need for a certain amount of financial provision. The Father already has the provision arranged. He spoke to someone to sow a seed into your life and that seed comes into your hand at just the right moment. Perhaps you suddenly had the opportunity to earn some extra cash and that is how He provided for you. Perhaps you suddenly got a rebate or refund unexpectedly that was the precise amount that you needed at that time. Or perhaps an inheritance was released to you that had been held up until that time. Is it possible if those funds had been released earlier, they would have been spent elsewhere and not where the Father had in mind? Heaven is not limited in how provision can manifest for you or in you.

Failure in the Tithe

When you receive your paycheck, the tithe is already assigned from those funds, additionally, offerings are assigned from those funds. Maybe part of the funds will help pay your mortgage, buy groceries, or make the car payment. Because it has an assignment, we need to make sure we co-labor with Heaven so that those funds go where they are intended by Heaven.

All money has an assignment.

When you make a purchase at a store, a portion of those funds are eventually intended to provide a paycheck to the workers in that store, which in turn provides tithe income, offerings, house payments, groceries, shoes, etc. Money has an assignment. Help it get distributed properly.

Your tithe is not to buy your children's shoes. It is not to buy groceries. It may be in *your* bank account, yet it does not belong to you. You are stewarding it for the family. It is the property of the Father, placed in your hands to teach you lessons of trust, faith, stewardship, and obedience (among other things). If you are petitioning for finances but have not been obedient to return the tithe to the storehouse to which you are assigned, the enemy can appeal your petition on those grounds. It is difficult for a farmer to have a harvest on seed that is not yet sown. Have we (as Malachi 3 says), robbed God with the tithe and/or offering? If I were farmer and I had plowed a field, planted the seed, and then cultivated it, I should have a reasonable expectation of harvest. The degree of harvest depends upon the quality of the field the seed is planted in.

For believers you want your seed planted:

Where you are assigned. You do not go shopping at one store and pay for the items at another store. If you are being fed from one location, but pay for it at another location, they have a word for that—stealing. If I went to a department store and picked up items, but did not pay for them at that store; rather, I took the items with me and paid the store down the street, they would consider that shoplifting. A lot of believers are shoplifters in that respect.

The promise of God in the tithe is that the devourer will be rebuked for your sake.

If your seed is being devoured, it may well be that the devourer has a legal license to rob and steal from you. Malachi 3 makes it plain.

Some will argue that all your money belongs to the Lord and that the tithe is not a New Testament concept. They would be right on both parts. All your money belongs to the Lord, not just the tenth which is the tithe. The Father is only asking for a tenth, not the whole amount, so what is the problem? Also, it is not a New Testament concept. It even pre-dated the Old Covenant described in the some of the Old Testament. It is first shown with Abel's tithe to the Lord in Genesis. Abraham tithed to Melchizedek. It is spoken of in Hebrews. It is not an Old Covenant concept nor is it a New Covenant concept. It predates the Old Covenant and supercedes the New Covenant.

Heaven does not consider the tithe as done away with by the cross.

It is Heaven's means of supporting the work and workers of the Kingdom, so their focus can be on the reception and release of revelation to grow the sons. The sons of God should be the most generous people on the planet. Like the early church recorded in Acts, their generosity should impact and change the culture in which we live.

The reason Mormons are able to accomplish so much and advertise so much is that approximately 80% of Mormons consistently tithe. The principles work whether you have everything altogether or not.

As a ministry, we have assignments and projects that we are to develop, fund, and grow. The funding for that is designed primarily to come through the faithful support of those the Father has assigned to join with us in our assignment. When the Father leads you or instructs you to join hands with a particular ministry, he does not assign your money to some other ministry that you may have formerly belonged to or your favorite TV preacher. The tithe belongs in the storehouse. A storehouse is a repository for food. Are you being fed by a particular ministry? Then prove it by your faithfulness to support it with your tithe.

On another note, if you are assigned to a particular ministry and for some reason you decide to separate yourself from that ministry, the tithe that would go to support that ministry is still assigned to where you are assigned, not necessarily where you attend. Until you are released from the ministry to which you are assigned, the tithe still belongs with that ministry and the leader of that ministry is not obligated to release you from the obligation.

Malachi 3:10 instructs us to bring ALL the tithe into the storehouse. We do not have any scriptural precedent for splitting the tithe between several different ministries.

In that passage, the Lord has promised to open the windows of Heaven (release revelation in abundance). According to Malachi 3:9, the whole nation is affected by the disobedience of one or a few. Certainly, not the entire nation was refusing to tithe, but because many were refusing to tithe, it impacted the entire nation. Verse 9 says,

> *You are cursed with a curse, for you have robbed me—the whole nation. When you refuse to tithe, you are not merely robbing God; you are also robbing your fellow sons. All are affected by obedience, and all are affected by disobedience.*

Many times, we face financial shortfalls because we have not been responsible stewards. The Father has a remedy for that, but it requires our obedience at the most basic of levels.

Lack of Faith

Earlier in this chapter we discussed one reason for appealing a petition, which was a lack of faith. As we grow in sonship, more and more of the religious mindsets that many of us still carry will be shed from us. The late apostle, Lester Sumrall, once defined faith as simply knowing God.

Numbers 23:19 tells us:

[19] God is not a man, that He should lie, nor a son of man, that He should repent. Has He said, and will He not do? Or has He spoken, and will He not make it good?

[20] Behold, I have received a command to bless; He has blessed, and I cannot reverse it.

Isaiah 55:9-11 says:

[9] For as the heavens are higher than the earth, so are My ways higher than your ways, and My thoughts than your thoughts. [10] For as the rain comes down, and the snow from heaven, and do not return there, but water the earth, and make it bring forth and bud, that it may give seed to the sower and bread to the eater, [11] so shall My word be that goes forth from My mouth; it shall not return to Me void, but it shall accomplish what I please, and it shall prosper in the thing for which I sent it.

We need to develop an unshakeable faith and confidence like Solomon who had seen the promise of God fulfilled in the children of Israel and recorded in 1 Kings 8:56:

> *Blessed be the LORD, who has given rest to His people Israel, according to all that He promised. There has not failed one word of all His good promise, which He promised through His servant Moses.*

Paul had an unshakeable faith as did Abraham and the others listed in Hebrews 11. May we, like Lester Sumrall, know God—He is not a man that He should lie.

According to Mark 11:22, it is not even *our* faith that we must have. We already possess faith originating from the Father. Do you suppose He has any trouble believing for anything? He and Jesus are not sitting in Heaven looking down at you and your situation and saying, "Oh my, we didn't see that coming! What are we going to do?"

No! Before there was ever a need for a need, the provision was already set aside and earmarked for you in Heaven. The supplication is part of the requisition process to get the resources of the Kingdom into your hand. You want to go from merely supplication to the acquisition of the thing you need.

False Narratives

If we are under the impression that we can enter this court without being honest and truthful, and without presenting a true narrative, then we are grossly mistaken. There can be no falsehood here. A supplication can be appealed because you are presenting false evidence. You must remember to mind your mouth. You cannot come into this court in intimacy and lie. You cannot present anything false in this court because of intimacy. There will be those that will try to enter this court one way and they will leave another. It is one thing to know that you are a son, but it is another thing to be arrogant about it.

For example, as we make a petition and we are only telling the favorable part of the story to the Court and not admitting our failures and repenting of them to the Court, we can expect an appeal by the enemy on our supplication. Presenting a false narrative is typically based on pride and not wanting to be seen as "less than" in other's eyes, but we must be transparent, telling the truth, the whole truth, and nothing but the truth (which is the oath one typically takes in the courts of law in the United States of America). One of the ten commandments is to not bear false witness (Exodus 20:16) and we would do well to remember that.

Hidden Motives

Heaven knows our motivations for doing what we do.

No secrets exist in Heaven.

For instance, there have been cases when someone would pray for a divorce between a married couple. However, the hidden motive was this: the one doing the praying was "in love" with one of the partners and wanted any opposition moved out of the way. You do not want that prayer to be answered because it is simply wrong on several accounts.

Asking Malcolm what some other hidden motives are, he gave me a scenario of the people in Heaven, who, without judging us, simply know everyone's motives in Heaven. If we could only realize that Heaven (and hell) know our motives. We cannot bring hidden motive into this court. We cannot operate with hidden motives. Heaven and hell know our motives.

Pride

We have already mentioned a bit about pride, but we must look at it from some other angles. Do we want to maintain our status or stature in front of others and do we want prayers answered that would reinforce that motivation? James 4:3 tells us that we may be asking and not receiving because we are asking for the wrong reason—we have the wrong motivation behind what we are doing.

If we want to keep up appearances of some sort, that is a demonstration of pride being involved. We do not want to be found wrong about a matter and so we operate in pride and will not allow the higher road of humility to be the one we travel. Instead, we travel the lower road of pride.

Proverbs 16:18-19 tells us:

> [18] *Pride goes before destruction, and a haughty spirit before a fall.*

19 Better to be of a humble spirit with the lowly, than to divide the spoil with the proud.

Humility must always be a part of our lives. As sons, we must understand that sonship is a privilege, and we cannot be arrogant about it. We have been graced by our heavenly Father to be called and adopted as sons. Let us not forget how that came about.

Frustration

When we present a petition in frustration, we can often be doing so out of a motivation to make things better for ourselves and not to benefit the other party.

When frustration is in operation, often love is not.

The word *frustrate* means to set aside, to cast off, or to disesteem. When we operate in frustration, we are not esteeming the other party. I have been guilty of this. I do not want it to be a regular practice, but it has happened. We may have a situation within the ministry where someone's actions are extremely frustrating, but when I realize that if I am reacting to frustration, I am disesteeming the other party, I am setting aside the other party or not hearing the real reason for their behavior. It takes grace to esteem them properly. Paul instructs us in Philippians 2:3:

> *Let nothing be done through selfish ambition or conceit, but in lowliness of mind let each **esteem others** better than himself. (Emphasis added)*

Let us be aware of the pit that frustration digs for all the parties involved and not let it be a part of our motivations in our petitions before the Lord.

Be assured that in this court, if you come in one way, you WILL leave another. We always want to be pliable before the Lord and subject to his instructions, not arrogant, not prideful, not a "know it all." A know it all really does not know as much as they like to think. Let us always rely on the one who knows all and sees all.

We have the promise of Mark 4:22:

> *For there is **nothing** hidden which will not be revealed, nor has anything been kept secret but that it **should come to light**. (Emphasis added)*

The same principle is found in Matthew 10:26, Luke 8:17, and Luke 12:2. We need not think our stuff can stay hidden.

We also have the promise of Psalm 9:8:

> *You have set our iniquities before You, our secret sins in the light of Your countenance.*

Let us own up to our junk and come before the courts with pure hearts borne of intimacy with the Father. It is all an outgrowth of intimacy.

Love is the motivator.

The enemy knows, and believe me—he will try to inflict such various challenges upon the sons to keep them from entering this place because he is not welcome.

Questioning if you hear God correctly when he speaks.

This is a form of a false narrative if we question our hearing of His voice. We must learn, as Elijah did, that the voice of the Lord may not thunder, but be extremely quiet. Whether we perceive by seeing, hearing, feeling, or knowing, we must develop a confidence that we know when Heaven is speaking.

The Apostle John described the process in 1 John 5:14-15:

> *Now this is the confidence that we have in Him, that if we ask anything according to His will, He hears us.* ¹⁵ *And if we know that He hears us, whatever we ask, we know that we have the petitions that we have asked of Him.*

If a petition is according to His will—He hears us. Therefore, if we know that He hears us, it is simply a matter of following the protocol of this court in order to see the answer manifest on earth.

Discord or Strife

We have discussed Lack of Agreement as one of the reasons, but we did not delve into the discord that may arise as a result. The enemy will be able to detect discord.

It is possible to disagree without being disagreeable. Of course, it is always helpful when we can agree, but sometimes we have to simply agree on the main things.

As a revelation releasing ministry, not everyone agrees with what we release. They are not required to, nor am I required to always agree with them. Hopefully though, we can still function together as we agree on the main things—those that are truly important. The enemy will use strife to cause things that were about to breakthrough to get derailed.

Personal Uncleanness of Heart

If we say we have no sin, we deceive ourselves and the truth is not in us.[5] If the truth is not in us—an automatic appeal will follow due to the unconfessed sin in our lives. Sin in our lives will result in an automatic appeal, therefore we want to live with a righteousness consciousness rather than a sin consciousness.

When driving on a long bridge, if you are focused on the guardrails on the bridge, you are much more likely to have an accident. If, however, you stay focused on the road in front of you, your journey will be safer.

Do not focus on the guardrails, simply focus on the road ahead.
---

[5] 1 John 1:8

If I am focused on 'not sinning,' I will invariably sin. Yet, if I focus on pleasing the Father, 'not sinning' will not be a problem.

Allowing Feelings to Interfere

You may have noticed that your feelings will deceive you—quite often, in fact. Many factors can affect our feelings, which is why it is important to live spirit forward and spirit first. Do not give the enemy any room to appeal your supplications. Keep your feelings in check. Stay spirit forward.

Lack of Proper Governing

Whether on a corporate level or a personal level, a lack of proper governing can result in appeals to our supplications. My book, *Working with Your Realms & Your Realm Angels*,[6] unveils how you can improve the governing within your own life.

A major part of governing on a personal level involves governing the whisperings of accusations, doubt, fear, or complaining.

Lack of Preparation

Our lack of preparation in preparing our supplications can result in an appeal. We need to be careful not to be too

---

[6] *Working with Your Realms & Your Realm Angels – Volume 1*. LifeSpring Publishing (2024).

hasty in creating our supplications. We must research legal precedents, not trying to rush the process for acquisition. Heaven has a protocol, and we would do well to honor it.

Don't Build on Another's Foundation

This is particularly in regard to intimacy. You must develop your own lifestyle of intimacy with the Father. We can learn from others, glean from their wisdom, and even copy them for a season, but we need to be working toward our own foundation, our own relationship with Father based on what we have come to know.

Don't Settle for Substitutes

Being willing to settle for substitute responses to our supplications can be grounds for appeal since we have not fully settled that we will not simply accept substitutes. We want only the plan of the Father for our lives and future...no substitutes.

Not Trusting God to Honor His Word

Unbelief is the simple word to explain what is happening when we do not trust God to honor His Word. We are not convinced of Numbers 23:19 which says,

> *God is not a man, that He should lie, Nor a son of man, that He should repent. Has He said, and will He not do? Or has He spoken, and will He not make it good?*

This position of our heart would create an automatic appeal against our supplications. The next verse is a wonderful follow-up promise:

If we confess our sins, He is faithful and just to forgive us our sins and to cleanse us from all unrighteousness. (1 John 1:9)

Let's follow verse 9 and not fall into the trap of verse 8. Both Heaven and hell will notice.

Do not allow hell to use issues such as those mentioned to cause your breakthrough to vanish. Heaven wants to answer on our behalf, we simply need to follow the protocol.

Chapter 4
Liens on Supplications

As we engaged Heaven in a session with a client, we asked to see the client's Ledger of Supplications. As we reviewed it, we saw that it had a lien against it and, therefore, could not be finalized. In this case, the supplication regarded agreements toward the father, but not all the children agreed with the mother for Heaven to move on the father's behalf. The supplication was based on Matthew 18:19:

> *Again, I say to you that if two of you agree on earth concerning anything that they ask, it will be done for them by My Father in heaven.*

Since the children were not in agreement with the mother, she needed someone else to come into agreement with her concerning the children's father. At that point, Stephanie and I came into agreement with her concerning the supplication creating a three-fold cord. Once we did so, we saw "Granted" written on the ledger concerning that supplication.

Not every supplication has to have an agreement to be granted. But for those that do, you want to find someone who will come into agreement with you and not back out of that agreement. Notice in the passage that says, "If two of you agree **on earth**" *(not heaven and earth)*, it will be done for them. In my experience with agreements and the principles of agreement, you want someone to agree who has faith that they are willing to couple with your faith in order to see a matter taken care of.

Some of us have said we would agree, but in a short span of time, we released our hold of faith on that agreement or by the words of our mouth came out of agreement, and the situation was never resolved the way Heaven intended. In the natural, when you create an agreement, the agreement is designed to stand until the matter around which the agreement is made gets resolved—typically by fulfillment of the terms of the agreement.

Heaven has made it simple. We only have to have two for an agreement to be made. It has to be made by people living on the earth, and it can be about any issue within the parameters of the will of the Father. Just as angels will not do something for you that is outside of the will of God for you, neither will Heaven work on your behalf for something outside of the Father's will for you.

In 1 John 5:14-15, we read:

[14] Now this is the confidence that we have in Him, that if we ask anything according to His will, He hears us. [15] And if we know that He hears us,

whatever we ask, we know that we have the petitions that we have asked of Him.

If we fulfill the protocols of a petition, it will be granted. If the particular petition requires agreement, then find someone who will come into agreement with you. If I were plowing a field, I would not want to be plowing with someone who would get halfway through, then just quit, saying, "I am done. I do not want to do this anymore!" and then walk off the job.

The writer of Amos, in chapter 3, verse 3, asks the question:

Can two walk together unless they are agreed?

But if you are in agreement, so much more can be done.

Heaven has interesting mathematics. In Heaven's economy, one can put a thousand enemies to flight, but two can put ten thousand to flight.[7] Agreement creates an exponential situation for those entering that agreement.

When we came into agreement with our client for the supplication at hand, the simple act of agreement with her caused the lien upon the supplication to be immediately removed. Unlike situations where liens can be upon people or property and the Court of Titles and Deeds is involved, this situation did not require their involvement. Whether that was because in this court, we had immediate access to other courts from the Court of Supplications and

---

[7] Deuteronomy 32:30

Acquisitions, I do not know, but it was interesting to see the immediate change in the status of the supplication once the conditions were met.

Heaven does not make obtaining answered prayers difficult. However, we must meet the conditions for the petitions we are presenting. A petition is simply an asking. A supplication is a petition with legal precedent (pertinent scriptures) attached as part of the overall supplication.

In this situation, our client also had prophetic words that had been spoken concerning the situation that she was holding on to. She asked if she could simply agree with those prophetic words. I suggested that she add those in conjunction with the scriptures that were attached to the supplication. Prophetic words, however legitimate, may not have the same standing as scripture, which is why I suggested she add them in conjunction with the Word.

Additionally, we learned that one son, who was seeking after the Lord, was in agreement with his mother in this matter, even though his other siblings were not in agreement. She attached his agreement to the agreement that the three of us had made earlier in the session, further strengthening the legal precedent in our client's favor.

Often in court cases, the initial paperwork will cite other court cases that show precedent for the case at hand and for the court to judge according to the legal precedent already established. You never want to be plowing new ground when it comes to a significant court case. You always want to have the strength of prior court rulings showing grounds for a positive response to a petition.

When we add scripture to a supplication, that is what we are doing. You may have heard me say that "past provision prophesies future provision." If God did it before, He will do it again in the future. The fact that you have been healed in the past demonstrates the Father's willingness to heal you in the future. The fact that you have had supernatural provision in the past sets a precedent for supernatural provision to be provided for you in the future.

Heaven did not indicate that we needed dozens of scriptures to see a supplication granted. One to three will do.

One or two will demonstrate precedent, and three will establish it.

It also moves our petition from one based on hope to one based on established facts. He provided for the Children of Israel for over 30 years in the desert. He can certainly provide for you and your family. It is not a stretch for the Father to do so; however, he does want you involved in the process. Many prayers have been based on hope instead of faith and therefore are sitting in limbo, waiting for faith to be attached to them so they can be fulfilled. What is the basis for your prayers?

Hidden Sins

In the chapter on appeals, we discussed hidden sins briefly. Simply said, hidden sins will invariably cause a lien to be placed against our supplication. The lien must be removed before the supplication can be granted. However, Heaven has made it extremely easy to get the lien removed through confession and repentance.

1 John 1:9 is key to a lien's removal:

If we confess our sins, He is faithful and just to forgive us our sins and to cleanse us from all unrighteousness.

Psalm 90:8 states:

You have set our iniquities before You, Our secret sins in the light of Your countenance.

From the above scriptures, we can see that our sins will be brought to light, and if we think we have no sin, we are in self-deception. However, freedom is not far away. Simply confess your sins—which is to say the same thing about your sin that God does.

Ask yourself:

- Does God approve of that secret sin—the one you think is hidden from everyone? God does not approve of us destroying ourselves or others by our behavior.
- Do you think you will always "get away with it"? The old saying, "Be sure your sin will find you

out," is true. Sometimes, it may take a while, but eventually it will be uncovered.
- Do you think you "get a pass" because you are so anointed?

When it comes to sinful behavior a principle is involved of seed, time, and harvest. I knew of a pastor who was highly anointed in the pulpit but outside the pulpit, he was committing adultery with numerous women in the church whom he was seducing. Even though he had committed adultery the week prior, he thought that God was excusing his behavior because he was still "anointed" when he ministered.

I asked Heaven about that and why he was still experiencing the anointing when he was ministering. He was married during this time, too!

Holy Spirit explained that when he was younger, he diligently sought the Lord. The harvest he was reaping by the present anointing was a result of seed sown in years past. He had not started reaping the harvest on the current seed he was sowing. Seed + Time = Harvest is a principle that always works. Never expect that it does not.

To avoid liens upon our supplications, repentance is crucial. We must not think that hell does not know about our junk. Supplications are a collaborative work between the sons of God and Heaven. Are we willing to confess our sins and have our supplications remain "lien free"? It is simple. Do you want your supplications to always be approved? Live clean.

Liens come from darkness because they know your secret sin but are easily overturned (1 John 1:9). People in positions of authority have the most trouble with this as they do not want to "lose face" with those they have oversight over.

Just as with the things that can create appeals on supplications, similar things can create liens. The secret to having "lien-free" supplications is humility. Have your heart right before the Lord.

Stephanie said to Malcolm, "You are saying that acknowledging that you are willing to do all this work in the Court of Supplications and Acquisitions is crucial, but there is one thing that you are holding onto that you are not willing to admit or repent for. Is that correct? I know people who will come back and say, 'Jesus died once and for all.'"

Malcolm replied, "He did. But this is a collaborative work between the sons and Heaven. Are you willing? The key to freedom is confessing your sins and repenting. The scripture says, "He's faithful and just to forgive you of our sins."[8]

Malcolm continued, "Nothing is hidden—nothing. People in positions of authority have the most trouble with this."

Stephanie replied, "I get it. Malcolm, you are saying pastors and ministers and others in authority are the ones

---

[8] 1 John 1:9

who feel like they must keep things hidden sometimes. Is there any other way that a lien can be put on someone else's life?"

He showed her that the lien comes from the kingdom of darkness because they know the secret sin that is just as easily overturned through confession. This is why it is so important to have your heart right before the Lord.

Malcolm explained, "This is humility at its finest."

———·———

Chapter 5

Access the Court Through Jesus

Stephanie asked, "Regarding individuals that have relationship with Jesus, how do we tell the people, many of whom have a problem of feeling unworthy of a relationship with Jesus, about this court and this process without making them feel that they're an outcast or become offended?"

The Magistrate replied, "Jesus will meet them at the door of this Court if they truly want a relationship. The entrance is *through* him. He accepts them when they come."

Stephanie remarked, "That's good to know. I was questioning about how we all step into the realms of Heaven through Jesus and this being different. Jesus is standing at the door of this Court to grant them entrance through relationship, whereas, when we come into the realms of Heaven, just because we are all accepted as sons, we are coming through Him there. But in this place, He's meeting us face to face."

Some scriptures came to mind.

Acts 1:14:

These all (the disciples) continued with one accord in prayer and supplication, with the women and Mary the mother of Jesus, and with His brothers.

Philippians 4:6:

Be anxious for nothing, but in everything by prayer and supplication, with thanksgiving, let your requests be made known to God.

Ephesians 6:18:

Praying always with all prayer and supplication in the Spirit, being watchful to this end with all perseverance and supplication for all the saints—

Stephanie asked if those scriptures could be placed on the front of the ledger. As she asked, the words appeared as I read those scriptures.

The Magistrate remarked, "Talk about authority!!!"

Because of our authority in Him, we are a part of the process of even obtaining justice in this court.

The Magistrate added, "Wait until you get to the Lamb's Supper and see what you get to do there."

Nothing else was on the docket for us that day, so Gloria left us with the words, "Continue to persevere."

We ended with a final petition from Psalm 19:14, saying, "I would like to add a supplication with that scripture, that those that draw near to LifeSpring, and especially those that contract with and work for LifeSpring and all components of LifeSpring, that the words of their mouth are acceptable to You, that no defilement comes from our mouths."

The Magistrate replied, "Granted."

Stephanie remarked, "Wow, that was easy. What is a scripture about discord?"

I replied, "Well, there is Proverbs 6. It talks about someone with perversion in his heart who devises evil continually. He sows discord, and then the Lord deals with it. Verse 19, the false witnesses who speak lies and one who sows discord among the brethren."

I rephrased it into a petition, "We want all discord cut off from the ministry among those who are employees, contractors or volunteers, those who track with us, those who are students in the FTP program or those who formerly tracked with us, those who are coming to any of our conferences, those that join us online, and those who take courses, in Jesus' name based on Proverbs 6 and Psalm 133:1:

> *Behold, how good and how pleasant it is for brethren to dwell together in unity!"*

The Magistrate responded, "Granted."

Stephanie exclaimed, "This is fun! I need to learn my scriptures more. I get the first words of it, and then I must go look it up."

The Magistrate replied, "It's part of the fun."

Stephanie remarked, "You sound like Ron!"

———— · ————

Chapter 6
Working Through Your Petitions

Not wanting to leave anything undone, I asked if we needed to add any scriptures or make any other supplications.

Stephanie heard Isaiah 54:17:

'No weapon formed against you shall prosper, and every tongue which rises against you in judgment You shall condemn. This is the heritage of the servants of the LORD, and their righteousness is from Me,' says the LORD.

Our petition was:

For those that are working against or speaking against what we are doing with LifeSpring, through the books, sessions, HDB, and Aftercare, that discordant voices be shut down and what they intend with their words would not bear fruit. Based on Isaiah 54:17.

Stephanie saw "Granted," and then she saw Isaiah 54:14-15:

¹⁴ In righteousness you shall be established; you shall be far from oppression, for you shall not fear; and from terror, for it shall not come near you. ¹⁵ Indeed they shall surely assemble, but not because of Me. Whoever assembles against you shall fall for your sake.

This petition was:

We request this supplication that there is no tyranny amongst the ranks because we have nothing to fear. And terror will be far removed, and it will not come near us. Whoever attacks us will surrender to us based on Isaiah 54:14-15.

Thinking of those people's children and grandchildren, Stephanie added, "I would like to add this supplication and verses for the ministry that many of us, in our ministry, have children that are far from the Lord. I would like to add as a supplication, on behalf of the ministry and all those that draw near, work for LifeSpring, etc., that we want our children to follow the Lord because in verse 13 it says, 'All your children will be taught by the Lord and great will be their peace.'"

Stephanie continued, "I want that for all of those that are out there, that are a part of this ministry, which are struggling with their children and their grandchildren, I would like for that to be as a supplication with that prayer behind it on all of our behalf."

The Magistrate stated, "Granted."

Stephanie continued, "I would like for everything that we have been given, revelation-wise, for us to be able to come into the full knowledge and understanding of that because some people read it, listen to it, and they don't absorb it, they're having trouble getting it, based on Ephesians 1:17-20, which states:

> [17] *that the God of our Lord Jesus Christ, the Father of glory, may give to you the spirit of wisdom and revelation in the knowledge of Him,* [18] *the eyes of your understanding being enlightened; that you may know what is the hope of His calling, what are the riches of the glory of His inheritance in the saints,* [19] *and what is the exceeding greatness of His power toward us who believe, according to the working of His mighty power* [20] *which He worked in Christ when He raised Him from the dead and seated Him at His right hand in the heavenly places.*

"And Ephesians 6:18-20:

> [18] *praying always with all prayer and supplication in the Spirit, being watchful to this end with all perseverance and supplication for all the saints—* [19] *and for me, that utterance may be given to me, that I may open my mouth boldly to make known the mystery of the gospel,* [20] *for which I am an ambassador in chains; that in it I may speak boldly, as I ought to speak."*

Stephanie added a current issue that we were experiencing with our emails. I suggested 2 Peter 1:3:

> *As His divine power has given to us all things that pertain to life and godliness, through the*

knowledge of Him who called us by glory and virtue.

We need our email system to work without trouble, without being defamed by being black-listed, gray-listed, or anything of the sort.

We worded our supplication like this, "That all our communications would be able to be delivered and received properly without trouble, without aggravation, without being gray-listed or black-listed. But that we will be able to communicate with those we need to communicate with as part of our means of operation for the ministry."

We added the scripture from Deuteronomy 28:7:

The LORD will cause your enemies who rise against you to be defeated before your face; they shall come out against you one way and flee before you seven ways.

And Exodus 23:22:

But if you indeed obey His voice and do all that I speak, then I will be an enemy to your enemies and an adversary to your adversaries.

The Magistrate replied, "That one became an immediate appeal."

Stephanie asked, "Why?" The word I heard from the enemy is that we did not search a matter out. Stephanie testified that circumstances with our email provider were beyond our control. According to Matthew 25, we came into agreement with the accuser that we did not search the matter out. We heard the gavel come down as forgiveness was granted to me.

Immediately, the appeal was stricken, and the petition moved back to the front of the ledger.

We were then impressed to request that the coffers of LifeSpring be filled according to Genesis 27:28:

> *May God give you the dew of Heaven and the fatness of the earth and plenty of grain and wine.*

And Proverbs 3:10,

> *Then your barns will be filled with plenty, and your vats will be bursting with wine.*

Stephanie prayed,

We request that our coffers be full on behalf of the ministry and those that draw near according to the scriptures just mentioned.

Stephanie asked, "What do you want the supplication to actually say?"

Our petition read:

We request that the coffers of LifeSpring be filled according to Proverbs 3:10, that the barns would be filled with plenty, and the vats be bursting with new wine. That Genesis 27:28 be applied, 'The due of heaven, the fatness of the earth and the plenty of the grain and wine' would be given to LifeSpring, in Jesus' name.

The Magistrate replied, "Granted. Made you work for that one, didn't we?"

Following the leading in our spirits, we quoted Deuteronomy 6:10-11,

> *[10] So it shall be, when the LORD your God brings you into the land of which He swore to your fathers, to Abraham, Isaac, and Jacob, to give you large and beautiful cities which you did not build, [11] houses full of all good things, which you did not fill, hewn-out wells which you did not dig, vineyards and olive trees which you did not plant—when you have eaten and are full.*

And Joshua 24:13:

> *I gave you land on which you had not labored in cities that you had not built. You dwell on them. You ate the food of vineyards and olive orchards that you did not plant.*

The petition read:

We request that you would provide for us houses that we did not build, cities we didn't dwell in, that you would expand our borders on every side, based on Isaiah 54, Stretching larger tents and spreading out our stakes so that we have everything that we need to do the Kingdom assignment that's before us based on these scriptures we just read. Joshua 24:13 and Deuteronomy 6:10-11, and to where you are going to use a big fish or fishes to help do this, these kingdom financiers that will come alongside. We ask this as a supplication with these scriptures.

Again, the Magistrate replied, "Granted."

Jesus then came forward and asked that we make a petition about him singing over us and the ministry.

Zephaniah 3:14-17:

The LORD your God in your midst, The Mighty One, will save; He will rejoice over you with gladness, He will quiet you with His love, He will rejoice over you with singing.

Our petition read,

Father, we would request that you would sing over everyone associated with LifeSpring, those who draw near, those who want to draw near, those who are hungry for the revelation that we are sharing, every volunteer, every employee, every contractor, in Jesus' name based on Zephaniah 3:14-17.

Jesus remarked, "That's a good one."

As Jesus walked away, he raised his right hand and said, "And the joy of the Lord is your strength!"

"What's the supplication for that?" Stephanie asked.

I replied, "That we would walk in the joy of the Lord, which is our strength. according to Nehemiah 8:10."

The Magistrate commented, "I already had that one written down; it is coming online as granted because of what Jesus just implemented."

I asked Stephanie, "How does that ledger page look now?"

Stephanie replied, "It's full."

The Magistrate instructed, "Come here on the days you see Gloria."

We replied, "Thank you, Magistrate. It was a pleasure. Thank you for teaching us today. Thank you, Gloria."

As he closed the book, Stephanie could see Ezekiel receiving instructions and he then departed to begin fulfilling the instructions.

———·———

Chapter 7
It's About Intimacy

As we continued to acquire information on the Court of Supplications and Acquisitions, we again stepped into the realms of Heaven through Jesus. We called upon the seven spirits of God and our angels and Gloria. We requested to meet again with the magistrate who taught us in the prior engagement and found ourselves in what looked like a restaurant. We noticed that our names were put on what looked like a waiting list like you have in a restaurant.

We were led to an outdoor table and could see Gloria at the head of the table. It was evening with lights hanging everywhere. It was quite beautiful.

As we sat in that peaceful environment, Gloria pushed a docket over to Stephanie. As she opened the folder, she could see supplications. We could see that all of them had been granted. We same many answered supplications in the folder.

Stephanie had a question for Gloria because several of the team or those connected to the LifeSpring team were suddenly sick in various manners. We had done a supplication with scriptures attached the day before.

Gloria's replied, "The attack always comes before the answer."

I had a question for Gloria. She somehow knew and encouraged me to ask.

I explained, "In Ephesians 6:18 it says, 'Praying with all prayer and supplication **in the spirit**.' What does that mean? Does that have to do with praying in the spirit? I would like some understanding of that."

Gloria asked, "Where do you receive things from?"

I answered, "Our spirit."

Gloria noted, "The *word* always has dual meanings."

Stephanie added, "Yes. *In the spirit*, like in tongues and in the spirit (i.e., with your spirit forward). The scripture says to worship him in spirit and truth. Is it the same concept, Gloria?"

Gloria replied, "Yes. Are all your prayers in tongues?"

I answered, "No. And not all prayers are in English."

I asked, "Are you going to be making a supplication while you're praying in tongues?"

Gloria replied, "Holy Spirit knows what he's doing."

Gloria continued, "The point about intimacy is—that is what is truly gained through this process. If you search a matter out, you will find it. When people are desperate enough (and they are), and they have an understanding that the word behind a supplication has power, they will search a matter out. Isn't that what you are supposed to be doing anyway?"

Stephanie replied, "Well, there is scripture, Gloria, about searching a matter out. I also know that you are to study to show yourselves approved."

I added, "Proverbs 25:2: 'It is the glory of God to conceal a matter but the honor of kings to search out a matter.'"

Stephanie commented, "Well, we are kings! Gloria, why are we in this space?"

Gloria replied, "The Magistrate's busy." That is why our names were placed on the waiting list.

Continuing to teach us, Gloria said, "Be in the spirit and you will rightly be able to divide the truth."

Isaiah 55:10-11 says:

> [10] *For as the rain comes down, and the snow from heaven, and do not return there, but water the earth, and make it bring forth and bud, that it may give seed to the sower and bread to the eater,* [11] *so shall My word be that goes forth from My mouth; it shall not return to Me void, but it shall accomplish what I please, and it shall prosper in the thing for which I sent it.*

Stephanie remarked, "Isn't it funny that people want the Word behind revelation, but they don't seek out a matter for themselves?"

Gloria replied, "That is true. He is calling his sons to intimacy, and this is a way to attain that."

I noted to Gloria, "I see where some will want to treat this like a vending machine. They put in their three scriptures, and they expect to get their candy out."

Gloria answered, "Let them, because when you pray the Word to the Father, what do you receive?"

Stephanie asked, "But what about disappointment if it doesn't work?"

Gloria responded, "Why wouldn't it work? Let us go back to the very beginning of yesterday. What is the substance of things hoped for?"

I replied, "Faith."

Gloria continued, "Faith backed with the Word in a supplication in prayer is answered."

(In a previous engagement, Jesus said, "It gives Him glory to answer a matter every time.")

We asked, "Are we in an era where we are going to see this manifest more and more?"

Gloria responded, "You might say that."

"Is revelation an era?" She asked.

Gloria continued, "There have been eras of time where a revelation was released. This is that time."

Stephanie asked, "Have there been times that revelation wasn't released?"

I reminded her of the time between Malachi and the book of Matthew that was four hundred years or so.

I had another question: "When you say prayer and supplication, explain that a little bit more for me because—isn't there always something behind what is said? Philippians 4:6 Paul said, 'But in everything about prayer and supplication with thanksgiving, let your request be known.' So thanksgiving is concerning the answer to come as if it is already present?"

Gloria asked, "What is the substance of things hoped for?"

I responded, "So we should view it as the prayer is already answered and the answer is in hand as you are making this supplication? Your posture just should be a matter of doing the paperwork as it is a matter of belief. Besides, Heaven already knows what we are asking before we ask it."

Gloria queried, "Why wouldn't you believe? Based on those principles. He is a good Father. It does bring Him glory."

I added, "And as you are seeing answers to prayer, you are no longer anxious."

Stephanie remarked, "I had asked Gloria about when people always say, 'Well, so-and-so could be healed if it was his will.' She turned fast and looked at me and said, 'It is His will. It has not been His will that has kept things from people. It has been the iniquity.'"

Stephanie added, "I feel like what you're saying is the next phase of what we're doing now, Gloria, because we've been diligent and because the revelation that has been given to us about cleaning up the iniquity on the generational line, that now we can have the things that are hoped for because of faith and because of His Word being spoken out. It is like it is an agreement, isn't it? We are coming into agreement with His Word."

Gloria replied, "His Word is already fulfilled. This is the application of it in faith. His Word behind your prayer and supplication, it is His will."

Stephanie commented, "So we have been taking the enemy's words into us about, 'Oh, it just wasn't His will to fix that or to heal that,' when in fact there were legal rights against us that prevented this, right?"

Gloria answered, "Oh, it is His pleasure."

Stephanie continued, "The things that are coming through this make sense to me. It is His pleasure to answer our prayers because His Word does not return void."

Numbers 23:19 says,

God is not a man, that He should lie, nor a son of man, that He should repent. Has He said, and will

He not do? Or has He spoken, and will He not make it good?

Stephanie added, "And because the legal rights are removed, we have the fullness of this, don't we?"

Gloria replied, "In full measure."

Stephanie paused to thank the Lord then turned her thoughts to the attack on our team members and their families. She asked Gloria what was going on with that.

She replied, "There's one thing when it comes to an individual and it's another thing when it's comes to a party of people."

I asked, "What is our strategy for that?"

Gloria said, "I thought you would never ask."

We got up and went to our Strategy Room. Above the door it said, "LifeSpring Strategy Room." As we entered, we could see all sorts of technologies in the room. Stephanie went to the map table and asked, "What is the strategy when it comes to a group versus an individual?"

Gloria asked, "What is a three-cord strand?"

Stephanie replied, "Well, I mean, I know it's not easily broken."

I added, "That would be us."

Gloria responded, "Yes, but what is a three-cord strand?"

I said, "It would be us, the people and Heaven. Is that right?"

Gloria said, "Invite the three-cord strand into the matter." (Matter has multiple meanings).

I began, "Alright. We invite the three-cord strand into this matter concerning the health and wholeness of those connected to LifeSpring."

Stephanie added, "According to the Scripture that 'by His stripes we are healed' (Isaiah 53 and 1 Peter 2:24, and John 10:10), that 'we can have life and that more abundantly.' We ask to be added here. And Exodus 23:25, 'He will take sickness away from us.'"

Stephanie noted a very interesting angel standing over the map. The map was illuminated from underneath. The angels were looking for a wormhole or door. While we watched, he pointed to a spot on the map and an angel came. He spoke to the angel that came about where he pointed, and that angel left through a type of wormhole in the map.

Stephanie asked, "Angel, can you tell me what just happened based on the active agreement of the three-cord strand, the prayer and supplication?"

He replied, "The heart of the matter has been accomplished. The heart of the matter—everything is about matter."

I noted, "Matter is the result of substance."

The angel added, "Faith is the substance of things hoped for."

I concluded, "Faith, plus substance, (His substance) produces matter."

The angel said, "The heart of the matter; it brings Him good pleasure and it glorifies Him."

Stephanie noted, "This angel is very striking. I see his face. It is stone, but it is a beautiful stone. He has very set features."

As the engagement ended, Gloria said, "You are going to be able to meet the magistrate the next time that we all meet."

We thanked her for her hospitality.

In closing, we asked if there was anything that she needed.

She replied, "Just your obedience."

Chapter 8
Your Personal Court of Supplications & Acquisitions

Our next engagement found us meeting with the magistrate in the Court of Supplications and Acquisitions. He began to speak, "Similarly to the personal Court of Records,[9] you have a personal Court of Supplications and Acquisitions because access to it is gained through intimacy. It is our personal courtroom in the very heart of the Father."

We have a personal courtroom in the heart of the Father—OUR Court of Supplications & Acquisitions

---

[9] We had discovered that each of us has a personal Court of Records. Everything about us has been recorded—much more than just the hairs on our head being numbered.

The magistrate said, "I, too, enjoy seeing the **heart of the matter**."

Stephanie noted, "'Matter' is a word with multiple meanings in this engagement because these supplications *matter* to the Lord, but also this is a tangible thing in His heart, made of *matter*."

The magistrate said, "I am your (personal) magistrate, and each will have their own. I come when I am called."

Stephanie commented on what she understood, "He comes, not because of me, but when I ask to enter, he comes because Jesus calls him. These are chambers within the very heart of the Father. I am now being taken out to a bird's eye view. The reality of this is within His heart, and I am being taken further and further out to witness a point of view.

"Now I understand why we saw that movie picture (in a previous encounter) with the Spirit of Wisdom creating the foundations of these places because they knew we would come.

It is not a court that everyone has access to because intimacy is required.

"This is *my* specific court. *You* have a specific chamber. These are chambers within this Court of Supplications. The angels created the foundations of these within the heart of the Father for each one of us, already knowing who would come and who would not. I just want to worship you Father, for including me and calling me, drawing me to this."

The magistrate said, "It still had to be an act of your will."

Stephanie replied, "Then, how did I get here—because I know me and my family, how did we get here? We were so vile."

The magistrate replied, "Everything good that is within you is because of Him."

Stephanie remarked, "We can't take any credit for anything here."

I added, "It is He that made us, not we ourselves."[10]

Stephanie, still at a distance because of the bird's-eye view she had been in, saw the magistrate closing the books, taking the gavel, turning around, and walking out of *my* chamber, *my* court, from within the chamber of the heart of the Father. *That is why it is intimacy that gets you in.*

Stephanie noted, "I am back on this mountain with this wind around me and the wind is making shapes of events of my life. I now have this understanding that I am watching the wind and the cloud form into shapes of

---

[10] Psalm 100:3, Know that the LORD, He *is* God; *it is* He *who* has made us, and **not we ourselves;** *we are* His people and the sheep of His pasture. (Emphasis added)

things that are in action right now—happening right now because *it is finished*.

"Wow. It is a whole new perspective of being accepted and sought after, especially for one who has been rejected—for all of those who have been rejected."

Chapter 9
Accessing Ease for Your Soul

As we were in this engagement, our souls were freaking out a little. You may be experiencing this as well. We knew about expanding our soul and requesting the oil of ease for our soul, so we paused to do that.

Gloria said, "Instruct your soul to embrace the ease from Heaven.

Instruct your soul to embrace the ease from Heaven.

"Embrace the revelation that's flowing because you're going to get to help a lot of people.

"Tell your soul, 'Soul, you will do great.'"

David's soul, which can be funny, said to him, "I was just getting used to the other stuff. Now you are making me go somewhere else!"

David then asked his soul, "Don't you prefer this over the stuffy religious stuff?"

To which his soul replied, "Well, now that you mention it, yes."

Speaking to his soul, David said, "You're made for this, soul. You can do this."

David had been thinking to himself that he was just helping because Stephanie was busy. He realized that this was a heavenly setup. What he was experiencing, how he was seeing scriptures—all that was going on.

He said, "I will never look at the scriptures the same way again. It is like the covers have been pulled off. I am sensing the weight, the necessity, and the reality of the Word of God all in one. Even though I look at Isaiah 46:10 often, when I read it earlier, it sounded different to me. It has a resonance or a different frequency than it seemed to have before."

Entering the Father's Heart

In Hebrews 4 we read of a place of rest. As I looked at that passage recently, I saw that he was possibly speaking of this place in His heart that was made for us. I will share the verses and interchange the word "rest" for "His heart." See how that explains some things as you read the following passage from Hebrews 4:1-13:

> *Therefore, since a promise remains of entering His rest [heart], let us fear lest any of you seem to have come short of it [2] For indeed the gospel was*

preached to us as well as to them; but the word which they heard did not profit them, not being mixed with faith in those who heard it. *³ For we who have believed do enter that rest [place in the Father's heart], as He has said: 'SO I SWORE IN MY WRATH, 'THEY SHALL NOT ENTER MY REST [heart],' although the works [chambers] were finished from the foundation of the world. ⁴ For He has spoken in a certain place of the seventh day in this way: 'AND GOD RESTED ON THE SEVENTH DAY FROM ALL HIS WORKS'; ⁵ and again in this place: 'THEY SHALL NOT ENTER MY REST [chamber of My heart].'*

⁶ Since therefore it remains that some must enter it, and those to whom it was first preached did not enter [the chamber of His heart] because of disobedience, ⁷ again He designates a certain day, saying in David, 'TODAY,' after such a long time, as it has been said: 'TODAY, IF YOU WILL HEAR HIS VOICE, DO NOT HARDEN YOUR HEARTS.' ⁸ For if Joshua had given them rest [a place in the Father's heart], then He would not afterward have spoken of another day. ⁹ There remains therefore a rest [place in the Father's heart] for the people of God. ¹⁰ For he who has entered His rest [heart] has himself also ceased from his works as God did from His.

¹¹ Let us therefore be diligent to enter that rest [place in the Father's heart], lest anyone fall according to the same example of disobedience. ¹² For the word of God is living and powerful, and

> *sharper than any two-edged sword, piercing even to the division of soul and spirit, and of joints and marrow, and is a discerner of the thoughts and intents of the (human) heart. ¹³ And there is no creature hidden from His sight, but all things are naked and open to the eyes of Him to whom we must give account. (Emphasis added)*

Do you see the richness of what the Father has provided in the chamber of His heart for us? Looking at this passage in this way helps unravel some aspects of it. It is through intimacy. As T.D. Jakes preached, the word "intimacy" is really "in-to-me-see." We must allow the Father access to ALL our heart–not just limited portions. It is in becoming vulnerable to Him in that manner that we become His friend.

Another passage that seems to clarify this is in Matthew 11:25-30:

> *At that time, Jesus answered and said, 'I thank You, Father, Lord of heaven and earth, that You have hidden these things from the wise and prudent and have revealed them to babes. ²⁶ Even so, Father, for so it seemed good in Your sight.*

> *²⁷ All things have been delivered to Me by My Father, and no one knows the Son except the Father. Nor does anyone know the Father except the Son, and **the one to whom the Son wills to reveal Him.** ²⁸ Come to Me, all you who labor and are heavy laden, and I will give you rest [a place in the Father's heart]. ²⁹ Take My yoke upon you and learn from Me, for I am gentle and lowly in heart,*

and you will find rest [a place in the Father's heart] for your souls. ³⁰ For My yoke is easy, and My burden is light.'

Applying this pattern to Isaiah 66:1-2, we see who qualifies for this place within the Father's heart:

*Thus says the LORD: 'Heaven is My throne, and earth is My footstool. Where is the house that you will build Me? And where is the place of My rest? [Where is that place in My heart?] ² For all those things My hand has made, and all those things exist [this place in My heart for you]," says the LORD. "But **on this one will I look**: on him who is **poor (humble)** and of **a contrite spirit**, and who **trembles at My word**.' (Emphasis added)*

And Isaiah 28:9-12:

'Whom will he teach knowledge? And whom will he make to understand the message?

'Those just weaned from milk? Those just drawn from the breasts? ¹⁰ For precept must be upon precept, precept upon precept, line upon line, line upon line, here a little, there a little.'

¹¹ For with stammering lips and another tongue He will speak to this people, ¹² to whom He said, 'This is the rest [the place within the Father's heart] with which You may cause the weary to rest [find a place in His heart],' and, 'This is the refreshing.'

This secret place has rich promises for us. In Isaiah 45:3, we read:

> *I will give you the treasures of darkness and hidden riches of **secret places** [within the Father's heart], that you may know that I, the LORD, who call you by your name, am the God of Israel.*

Within this place of intimacy, Father will share secrets and truths that will propel us to new places in our walk with Him. When He calls us by our name, that is an expression of intimacy.

Much of our prayer life has been exercised in the arena of our soul and not our spirit. With the concept of entering into our personal chamber of the Father's heart, take a look at these verses in Matthew 6:5-15:

> *And **when you pray,** you shall not be like the hypocrites. For they love to pray standing in the synagogues and on the corners of the streets, that they may be seen by men. Assuredly, I say to you, they have their reward.*
>
> *⁶ But you, when you pray, go into your [personal court] room [within the Father's heart], and when you have shut your door, pray to your Father who is in **the secret place**; and your Father who sees in secret [your intimacy with Him in this chamber] will reward you openly (acquisitions).*
>
> *⁷ And when you pray, do not use vain repetitions as the heathen do [do not pray from your soul]. For they think that they will be heard for their many words. ⁸ Therefore **do not be like them. For your Father knows the things you have need of before you ask Him.***

⁹ In this manner, therefore, pray [spirit forward and from within the Court of Supplications and Acquisitions]:

Our Father in Heaven, hallowed be Your name. ¹⁰ Your kingdom come. Your will be done on earth as it is in Heaven.

¹¹ Give us this day our daily bread.

¹² And forgive us our debts, as we forgive our debtors.

¹³ And do not lead us into temptation but deliver us from the evil one.

For Yours is the Kingdom and the power and the glory forever. Amen.

¹⁴ For if you forgive men their trespasses, your heavenly Father will also forgive you. ¹⁵ But if you do not forgive men their trespasses, neither will your Father forgive your trespasses. (Emphasis added)

Do you see how this is a description of what we have learned about the Court of Supplications and Acquisitions? It is so much richer than we have previously imagined.

When people are in close relationship with one another, they learn one another's nuances and idiosyncrasies. They often eventually learn to anticipate the other person's actions and even what they might say. It is natural in friendship for that to occur. Verse 8 tells us:

For your Father knows the things you have need of before you ask Him.

The Father can do more than simply anticipate. He even writes our petitions in our Ledger of Supplication for us to complete in due time. It is from this friendship that governing will arise.

———·———

Chapter 10
Accessing Your Mountain of Intimacy

As we engaged Heaven again, we were immediately translated from our chamber within the heart of the Father to a mountain. This mountain is different from our personal mountain where rulership takes place, although it contains elements of rulership.

In the Gospels, we read that Jesus went up to a mountain to pray. He was accessing this place.

Jesus was present with us in the chamber, and we wanted to know where that mountain of the Lord was.

We asked, "What is this governing ruling seat of authority?"

Jesus said, "Many do not recognize their seat of authority."

We then asked, "Jesus, is this different from the mountain that we have as our own mountain?"

He said, "It is different. Access to this mountain is also through intimacy—a mountain of the Lord."

Stephanie asked, "Will you give me more understanding, Jesus, of how this fits with the chamber of the heart of the Father and the Court of Supplications?"

He replied, "Are you not a ruling authority with my Word?"

She responded, "Your word is the final authority, Jesus."

He asked, "Did I meet you here, friend-to-friend?"

We replied, "Yes. "

He said, "Ask anything, and it shall be given to you."

Stephanie remarked, "Well, Jesus, I go back to that first time where I asked that Wisdom be able to walk through this life with me. I also have all these prayers about my life. How does this affect the people?"

He said, "Through one, it affects all. This is just an example. Speak my Word."

Stephanie noted, "I feel like this is where I can talk to Jesus as a friend and receive what he has to say in the situation. Jesus, I feel like we have done this, not from this mountaintop, but where we have used your Word."

He said, "This is your seat of authority on the mountain of the Lord. Regarding the ministry, what would be your authority? What would you pray here? Upon this rock, I will build my church."

Stephanie commented, "This is to me, Jesus, where I would want to go before I went to the Court of Strategy."

He said, "Strategies are strategies. This is My Word and authority upon the mountain of the Lord."

In scripture, when Jesus went up to the mountain of the Lord, it indicated a place where he would step into Heaven and engage with the Father. It is our place of engagement with the Father, but it may not be as deep as the chamber of his heart.

Not everyone experiences the mountain of the Lord. It requires deep intimacy. It is their choice. It is about a seat of authority. The mountain of the Lord is a gate.

Jesus said,

Rule with me. It is a measure.

"Speak the words that I give you here in the mountain of the Lord. It is bigger than the strategy room. This is coming directly to you, friend-to-friend, in this place—The Mountain of the Lord."

From here (the mountain of the Lord), authority comes.

Some people cannot get to this place and to the point where they are speaking what He is saying because of the lack of intimacy. They can stay in the strategy room.

Let us take a look at Isaiah 2:3:

> *Many people shall come and say, 'Come, and let us go up to the mountain of the LORD, to the house of the God of Jacob; He will teach us His ways, and we shall walk in His paths.' For out of Zion shall go forth the law, and the word of the LORD from Jerusalem.*

Let us be of the many people who go up to the mountain of the Lord. Now let us look at verse 2:

> *Now it shall come to pass in the latter days that the mountain of the LORD's house shall be established on the top of the mountains and shall be exalted above the hills; and all nations shall flow to it.*

This is an earned position because of walking with the Father, obeying, going through things, and character building.

The Father's heart is for all to reach this.

It is his desire, his yearning. It is attainable. It is a narrow road. It is your will. It is by choice. Choose whom this day you will serve. It starts there.

In Exodus 25:40, we see a principle that is laid out several times in the Word. Moses went up the mountain and while spending time with the Father, he was given blueprints for the tabernacle. He was told, "Make them according to the pattern shown to you on the mountain." This principle is repeated in Exodus 26:30, 39:42-43, Numbers 8:4, 1 Chronicles 28:11, and more.

On the mountain, Moses received instruction as a friend, including a glimpse at what the Kingdom of God on earth would be like (the Ten Commandments[11]), the blueprint for the Tabernacle, and much more.

He was given everything on the mountain. That is where he would go in intimacy. He built enough intimacy that the Father showed himself to him in several ways. That is where he received instruction. When Moses, in anger, struck the rock and the Lord did not allow him to go into the promised land, it was because he had an intimate relationship with the Father, and he knew better.[12]

2 Peter 1:17-19:

For He (Jesus) received from God the Father honor and glory when such a voice came to Him from the Excellent Glory: 'This is My beloved Son, in whom I am well pleased.' 18 And we heard this voice which came from Heaven when we were with Him on the holy mountain. 19 And so we have the prophetic word confirmed, which you do well to heed as a light that shines in a dark place, until the day dawns and the morning star rises in your hearts.

From the mountain of the Lord, we gain instruction and insight. The Strategy Room is where we can gain information and methodologies to deal with enemies and

---

[11] The Ten Commandments are an explanation of what life would be like (as Kingdom sons) absent the ten things listed.

[12] Numbers 20:10-12

situations, but the mountain of the Lord is more than that. It is not focused on the enemy; it is focused on intimacy. It is building us as we spend time with the Father.

The mountain of the Lord is within the chamber of His heart. That is where you meet friend-to-friend. Earlier in the book I mentioned how, from the Court of Supplications, we had immediate access to other courts to conduct business for situations. In that place, the Father said to "mind your mouth" and "the enemy is not welcome." The enemy cannot come into His heart.

It is truly from that place that we can govern. We can say we will have no division, no sickness, no chaos, and it will be so. It is governing on a much deeper level—from within the heart of the Father. This is where Job 22:38 comes into play:

You will also declare a thing, and it will be established for you; so light will shine on your ways.

From this place, you must be careful with your words, for you will have what you say.

The mountain of the Lord is not so much a separate place from the chamber of the Father's heart but rather an overlay on the chamber of the Father's heart.

You cannot think 3-dimensionally concerning this. The mountain of the Lord is within the Lord. It is within Him. The chamber is in His heart. We arrive on the mountain through the chamber, through intimacy. Jesus is the door into the Court of Supplications through intimacy, and from there, you go to the mountain.

———·———

Chapter 11
Run With It

Continuing to press in for more understanding, I contacted David, a colleague on our team at LifeSpring, to engage Heaven with me. As we stepped into the Courts of Heaven, we were led down a hallway into a classroom. It was David's first time in this classroom. Malcolm appeared, as he often does to tutor us.

Malcolm suggested we first look at timeframes, since, on earth, they are important. Our question was, "When one has a window of time in which a provision is needed, how do we go about submitting that to this court?"

Philippians 4:19 (My God shall supply all your need according to His riches in Glory by Christ Jesus) came to mind.

We asked, "How does that relate to a supplication?"

Malcolm said, "The person must first believe that the Word of God is *forever settled* in Heaven. So here in

Heaven, it is done. Everything is done in faith that **you have access** *and* **resources** available to you."

David asked, "How does that play out, Malcolm?"

David then asked for a definition of supplication, which is a petition with Scripture added that serves as the legal precedent for the request. If you went to court to obtain a verdict, you would present the request (a petition) with scriptures showing it is the will of the Father to provide that thing requested on your behalf. It gives a legal precedent for Heaven to do that or a similar thing again. You are saying, "I want a verdict in this kind," then you show other cases where they already granted that same kind of request. That provides legal precedent for them to do it again. In this case, Philippians 4:19 shows the legal precedent for the resources to be released from Heaven in a situation.

David then asked, "Once that is established, what does one do after that? Is the situation with Daniel, where he prayed for 21 days considered a legal precedent? In that situation, where the prayer was answered when Daniel prayed, but the receipt of the answer was held up, how do we handle that? What are our options?"

Malcolm explained, "This is when you employ angels to the fulfilling of the supplication to carry it out in the earth realm. Once the supplication is made—once the legal grounds are established, **you still must stand in faith** until it manifests. Faith is not taken out of the equation.

"Many times, what happens is—from the time that it is released until the time it is manifest, a person moves out of faith."

"Why is that, Malcolm? David asked.

He replied, "Because humans look at time. Faith is in the "**now** you have it." **Now** you receive it—now. Yes, there seems to be a lapse from the time you request a thing until it manifests in your life, but you do not operate from that place. You operate from Heaven down. You operate from spirit forward.

"You must understand that **you receive it now**, and even though you do not physically see or possess it, you possess it in faith, and you must hold onto that position and that mindset."

Hebrews 11:1 reads,

Faith is the substance of things hoped for and the evidence of things not seen. What does that mean to you?

David replied, "Well, faith is substance, and it also **releases evidence**."

Malcolm remarked, "So you have evidence, but you do not see it. Is that right?"

David answered, "Yes, I have evidence."

Malcolm continued, "There must be an aligning of your realms with the frequencies of Heaven as it relates to the legal precedent. Once something is settled—once something is ruled on in Heaven, it is done. It does not have to be redone. There is no need to redo."

Wanting to understand it more fully, David asked Malcolm to explain it another way.

He replied, "When you receive an answer based on the supplication, the only way to add to it is to do an amendment. But if you have received it the first time, go with it."

At that point, David heard, "We walk by faith and not by sight" (2 Corinthians 5:7) and Hebrews 11:6:

*But without faith it is impossible to please Him, for he who comes to God must believe that He is, and that **He is a rewarder** of those who diligently seek Him.*

While David was hearing these scriptures, he was praying in the Spirit. Because we can make petitions and supplications by praying in a known language AND by praying in the spirit, I asked if he could simply pray in the spirit until the knowing that the supplication was granted was alive within his spirit and that he has the breakthrough concerning that particular supplication.

Malcolm affirmed that it would be helpful and that it was what he meant by aligning. When you are praying in the spirit, you are bypassing the soul, and it can catch up to where your spirit is later. Your soul may be saying, "I don't know what to do," but your spirit has already taken care of the situation.

David thanked Malcolm for the insights, and Malcolm reminded him saying, "David, you are aware of this, but like many, you must maintain your posture in your spirit. This situation is not a surprise in your spirit. When you quote the scripture in Psalms 139:16 about the book that is written of you, you then align yourself with the book that is written of you. The Father is not surprised about anything that has happened. Remember that he is waiting for you to do just what you are doing now, to come into a new revelation, to come into an awareness, and then begin to execute these principles.

"We've been waiting for the sons to properly posture and align themselves with what Heaven has already put in place for them. There is nothing lacking, there is nothing missing, and there is nothing broken here. The sons must understand that the Kingdom of God is to come on earth just like it is here (in Heaven).

"David, how many times have you said that you confess that all your needs are met? Is that a supplication? Do you base it on the Word of God or scripture?"

"Yes," David replied, "I have."

Malcolm continued, "Pray in the Holy Spirit. Supplication activates acquisition.

Supplication activates acquisition.

"When you properly identify the legal precedents, the acquisition is the next step. You have acquired the right based on a legal precedent to receive and acquire what you have requested and what the Father has made available."

For clarification, I asked Malcolm, "Could it be said that the supplication provides the requisition resulting in the acquisition?"

Supplication provides the requisition resulting in the acquisition.

He said, "You have got it. That is the process. It is the request *with* precedent that creates the requisition, resulting in acquisition."

In 1 John 5, the Apostle John wrote:

> *Now this is the confidence that we have in Him, that if we ask anything according to His will, He hears us.* [15] *and if we know that He hears us, whatever we ask, we know that we have the petitions that we have asked of Him. (Emphasis added)*

Malcolm asked, "If you ask your father for a fish, will he give you a stone? Will your father not give good things to those who ask him (Matthew 7:7-11)?"

I asked if we could go into the Court of Supplications and Acquisitions so David could see his Ledger of Supplications so he can see how this works out in the fulfillment process.

We left the classroom to go to the court where David asked the magistrate for permission to see his ledger. He also asked if the magistrate would tutor him in understanding the ledger and the process.

David had a dear friend who had passed away earlier that week, and he desired to attend the funeral, which was going to be in Cincinnati, Ohio, in a few days. He needed provision released to him for the costs of the trip.

In the ledger, he saw "Cincinnati," and he saw "travel." I asked, "Do you see a scripture precedent listed with that situation?

David could not see the scripture listed providing precedent for the petition yet. He said, "I can't say I see the word 'Granted' yet. If it is not granted, what do I need to do so this *is* granted?"

While he was receiving a response from the magistrate, I felt the need to mention to him the scripture on the wall behind the magistrate's desk from Psalm 19:14:

Let the words of my mouth and the meditation of my heart Be acceptable in Your sight, O LORD, my strength, and my Redeemer.

I had been told repeatedly that we must watch what we say because that is what we will end up with so if we have said anything contrary to the provision manifesting, we would need to repent for that.

Immediately, David repented, saying, "I repent, Father, for anything I have thought, anything I have said in agitation or frustration. I repent for entertaining disappointment."

Then he said, "Okay, now I see the word 'Granted.'"

I suggested he look at the ledger to see when the petition was first entered into his ledger. As he looked, he realized it had been several years. I heard "Seven years."

I said, "It was already on the books, waiting for the need to arise. Remember, the Word says the Father knows what things you have need of even before you ask him...even before you even knew that you were going to have a need for it."

"Now look at your book and see if there is some other scripture or other legal precedent needed."

David heard Isaiah 46:10 about the power of confession:

> *Declaring the end from the beginning, and from ancient times things that are not yet done, saying, 'My counsel shall stand, and I will do all My pleasure,'*

David said, "I have been confessing that scripture for years; 'He declared the end from the beginning before ancient times of things that are not yet done.'"

I suggested he do a prophetic act to pull those resources into his life—from Heaven into the earthly realm.

As he did so, David could feel within him strength, confidence, and knowing that this was accomplished.

I then asked him, "If somebody's going on a trip, what would they do in the natural?"

He replied, "Start packing."

I added, "How the Father works it out is not your business."

David confessed that this process explained so much. He had been hearing and experiencing an ongoing whispering. He had been shutting it down over and over.

I said, "You need to use your realm angel over your soul to captivate those thoughts and whisperings, dispose of them and bring them into captivity to the obedience of the anointing (2 Corinthians 10:5)."

Immediately, David began to do that, saying:

I commission my soul realm angels now to bring every thought captive in Jesus, every whisper against the Father, against the goodness of God, every accusation that is against me, against His provision for me, and His love for me.

David then asked the magistrate if he would like to teach us anything else. He replied, "Life and death are in the power of your tongue. Heaven is aware of the onslaught that has been launched against you, but greater is the one who is in you than he who is in the world (1 John 4:4). That is why Jesus told you a few days ago to enter his rest."

David said, "That's what I have been saying since Tuesday. 'Jesus, I enter into your rest.'"

The magistrate continued, "You can come here and see your book. This is just the first step. This is just the beginning. There is so much more that the Father has designed for his children—for His sons. He is mindful of every son. He is mindful of every child. So mindful that that is why the number of hairs, the hairs on your head are numbered."

I suggested that David meditate on all this for a bit, pray in the Spirit and let it get deep inside his spirit and soul.

David replied, "I feel like I am on fire or something. Something has been ignited inside of me. Wow. Wow. Thank you, magistrate. Thank you, Malcolm."

I heard Malcolm say, "Run with this. Run with this. Pray in the spirit. Get your posture firmly rooted.

He Knows the Need

Later that same day we were meeting with a woman considering our Facilitator Training Program. I asked if she felt firmly that it was in the plans of the Father for her life. She affirmed that she did, so I suggested to her and Jeremy Friedman, another colleague, that we step into the Court of Supplications and Acquisitions to see her Ledger of Supplications.

As we stepped, she took a place standing behind Jeremy, who was looking over the magistrate's shoulder. I asked Jeremy to look at the ledger and see if he saw anything about this need. He could see the words Facilitator's Training.

We felt the need to add scriptures to the petition to create the full supplication. We prayed like this:

On behalf of our client, who believes it is the will of the Father for her to take part in the FTP[13] program and your word says in 2 Peter 1:3:

> *His divine power has given to us all things that pertain to life and godliness, through the knowledge of Him who called us by glory and virtue....*

And Philippians 4:19:

> *My God shall supply all your need according to His riches in Glory by Christ Jesus.*

Jeremy and I come into agreement with our client for this provision to manifest, based on Matthew 18:19:

> *If two of you agree on earth concerning anything that they ask, it will be done for them by My Father in Heaven.*

We thank you, Father, for taking care of our client in your perfect timing.

I then said to Jeremy, "There is a ledger book with all the different petitions that she has made. There is a box being highlighted that says 'Facilitator Training.'"

---

[13] FTP is our 11-month Facilitator Training Program where we teach people in the Courts of Heaven Prayer Paradigm. See ronhorner.com for more information.

I asked, "Is there anything that needs to be done for that particular petition?"

He asked the magistrate who said, "No, there is not. It has already been done."

Jeremy could see the word "Granted" written beside the supplication.

I said to Jeremy, "Take a look at the date when this was first entered in the ledger."

He replied, "It looks like November 2023."

Speaking to our client, I said, "That prayer of your heart was recorded in November 2023 into the ledger book and has been waiting for you to catch up to it. He knows what we need before we even ask Him."[14]

---

[14] Matthew 6:8

Chapter 12
Future Adjudication

We are just now learning about the quantum realm and the reality of quantum mechanics. One of the arenas that is most interesting is the arena of time and the impact of quantum understandings on time. The Father exists outside of time, which was created for our benefit so we would not exhaust ourselves from constantly operating our physical body in a particular time frame.

In Matthew 6:8, we read that the Father knows what things you have need of even before you ask him.

Even before we are aware of the need, the petition is already recorded in our Ledger of Supplications. We have seen that in the Ledger in our experiences in the Court of Supplications and Acquisitions. In one case, seven years prior, the petition was first recorded. When we checked the Ledger during the writing of this book, we saw it recorded. Originally, it was greyed out, indicating the person did not yet pray it, but it was recorded nonetheless, awaiting the need to become manifest in their realms.

That should bolster our faith to know the Father really does note the things you were going to have need of long before the need manifested much less the provision for the need.

I am reminded of a story of a medical clinic on the continent of Africa that had an important piece of equipment break. As the team of medical missionaries went to pray for a solution to the situation, a package was delivered to the clinic. Opening the package, they found it contained the exact piece of equipment that would replace the one that had broken. As they looked at the date of the postmark on the package, they discovered the package had been shipped several months prior to that day. The Father, in His goodness, had put on the hearts of some intercessors to purchase and ship a particular item to this clinic months before the need arose within the clinic for a replacement item. It was another demonstration of Matthew 6:8.

The Aspect of Time

Another of the aspects of sonship is to know we are not limited by time. We can step into the realms of Heaven and bypass the restrictions of time. We can step into the Court of Times and Seasons, see a timeline and step ahead into it, or step backward on the timeline to some point in the past. We can, by proper work in the courts, see wrinkles, splices, or other aberrations in a timeline corrected. The amendment to court cases of "As if it never were" can also be quite helpful in remedying things that have been affected by actions of the past.

As we inquired about stepping ahead into time to make a supplication, we were instructed that just as you establish legal precedent for a petition in this realm, you must establish legal precedent for stepping into the future. Everything is eternal.

We were directed to Isaiah 46:10:

Declaring the end from the beginning, and from ancient times things that are not yet done, saying, 'My counsel shall stand, and I will do all My pleasure,' [11] calling a bird of prey from the east, the man who executes My counsel, from a far country. Indeed, I have spoken it; I will also bring it to pass. I have purposed it; I will also do it.

Since, according to Psalm 37:23:

The steps of a mighty man are ordered by the LORD, and He delights in his way.

We have orders already. Orders are instructions. The orders are set as a blueprint of your steps, your next steps, your future steps...even tomorrow. Everything in our future has already been declared through the Word of God, so everything in our future is already in our past.

---

*Everything in our future
is already in our past.*

We are actually living in the past every day.

We have permission to step into the future at any time.

As we were learning this, we found ourselves in the future where George, our Financial Advisor, brought a stack of paperwork before David with a list of things that are in the blueprint for LifeSpring. Within LifeSpring, David is responsible for Accounts Payable, whereas Adina (my wife) is responsible for Accounts Receivable. Because of David's position in LifeSpring, I authorized him to read the blueprint aloud. Once we added scriptures to the petition, it would become a supplication, resulting automatically in a requisition in Heaven, for delivery to the earth.

The list included properties, bank accounts, personnel—things related to our blueprint and scrolls—and much more. As we acknowledged the various bank accounts, the amounts within them began to grow.

We added 2 Peter 1:3-4:

> [3] *...as His divine power has given to us all things that pertain to life and godliness, through the knowledge of Him who called us by glory and virtue,* [4] *by which have been given to us exceedingly great and precious promises, that through these you may be partakers of the divine nature, having escaped the corruption that is in the world through lust.*

And, of course, Philippians 4:19:

And my God shall supply all your need according to His riches in glory by Christ Jesus.

And Philippians 2:13:

...for it is God who works in you both to will and to do for His good pleasure.

As well as Ephesians 2:10:

For we are His workmanship, created in Christ Jesus for good works, which God prepared beforehand that we should walk in them.

We added Psalm 139:16-18:

[16] Your eyes saw my substance, being yet unformed. And in Your book, they all were written, the days fashioned for me, when as yet there were none of them. [17] How precious also are Your thoughts to me, O God! How great is the sum of them! [18] If I should count them, they would be more in number than the sand; when I awake, I am still with You.

George reminded us that once these items were signed off on, angels would be commissioned to carry them out. He explained that it was important that we acknowledge these things so they can be established on the earth.

David and I chose to verbally come into agreement with what George had shown us based on Matthew 18:19.

As we verbally agreed, the petition that had become a supplication became a requisition with which we agreed. David had seen what appeared to be an enormous warehouse where everything petitioned was stored, with the address of where it was to be sent and was simply waiting to be put out for delivery.

Another scripture to apply comes from Isaiah 55:10-13:

[10] For as the rain and the snow come down from heaven and do not return there but water the earth, making it bring forth and sprout, giving seed to the sower and bread to the eater, [11] so shall my word be that goes out from my mouth; it shall not return to me empty, but it shall accomplish that which I purpose, and shall succeed in the thing for which I sent it.

[12] For you shall go out in joy and be led forth in peace; the mountains and the hills before you shall break forth into singing, and all the trees of the field shall clap their hands. [13] Instead of the thorn shall come up the cypress; instead of the brier shall come up the myrtle; and it shall make a name for the LORD, an everlasting sign that shall not be cut off.

———·———

Chapter 13

Basic Rules for Supplications

In the Preface, I shared these Basic Rules for Supplications. In this chapter, I am going to expand on them based on what Angela, a woman in white who assisted in this portion, and Gloria, our legal counsel, shared with us.

David Porter and I engaged Heaven, asking for more information about this book. Angela came forward and told me to look at what I had just finished typing out (which was this listing). She began to expand it with additional scriptures. I will be discussing these additions here, so that we can more fully engage in the process.

Point #1:

Make your request in faith (Hebrews 11:6)

We will never get away from utilizing faith. No matter where we are. Some might say we will not need faith in

Heaven. Is that necessarily so? We shall find out at some point for sure!

The writer of Hebrews discusses the subject of faith in chapter 11 and informs us that if we want to please God, faith must be in operation. The verse reads:

> But **without faith,** it is impossible to please and be satisfactory to Him. For whoever would come near to God must [necessarily] believe that God exists and that He is the rewarder of those who earnestly and diligently seek Him [out]. (AMP)

If you are making a request of someone, you must have a reasonable expectation that the one you are asking has the available resources to supply your request.

Point #2:

Make your request according to the will of God.

Is it in alignment with the Word of God? James 4:3 describes a reason some prayers go unanswered:

> You ask and do not receive, because you ask amiss, that you may spend it on your pleasures.

The Apostle John said it well in 1 John 5:14-15:

> ¹⁴ Now this is the confidence that we have in Him, that if **we ask anything according to His will, He hears us**. ¹⁵ And if we know that He hears us, whatever we ask, we know that we have the petitions that we have asked of Him.

Philippians 1:6 was added to the list, which says:

...being confident of this very thing, that He who has begun a good work in you will complete it until the day of Jesus Christ....

Point #3:

Have scriptural precedent to support your petition.

It is a lot easier to have confidence in a prayer when you know that somewhere in the Bible, you will find scriptural precedent for your request. Some things we may not find a specific scripture but may find one that fits the general concept.

For instance, You will not find a scripture telling you to buy a Hyundai vehicle. The word Hyundai is simply not in the Bible. But you can find other scriptures that may support the receiving of the provision for your transportation, and the fact that you may particularly like a certain model Hyundai may simply be a matter of personal preference, which would fall under the category of a desire of your heart.

Point #4:

If you come into agreement, do not come out!

Matthew 18:19 shows us the power of agreement. Elsewhere in this book, I talk about the power of agreement. It only takes two people on earth to seal an agreement. See it through to the full manifestation.

If I say I will agree with you, I will do just that. I will extend my faith and add it to yours to see the fulfillment of what we are agreeing for. The object of the agreement is not even the issue. It is simply that I have given my word to you, and I will keep it. I learned that from my Dad to whom it was very important that you always kept your word.

Point #5:

Give thanks for the "already done" supplication because it IS already done!

Proverbs 3:5-6 speaks to the posture of the heart:

> *^{6} In all your ways acknowledge Him, And He shall direct your paths. ^{7} Do not be wise in your own eyes; Fear the LORD and depart from evil.*

Be careful what you say—even the position of your heart. There must be NO place where the supplication cannot be granted. That is why it must be based on the Word of God. There must be no place in a supplication where it cannot be granted. That is why it must be based on the Word of God and setting the precedent sets things in order in this court. You must be mindful of how you proceed and how you operate. Proverbs 16:3 instructs us:

> *Commit your works to the LORD, and your thoughts will be established.*

How you operate and the precedents you set are very important.

Point #6:

Understand the Purpose

Proverbs 8:21 reads:

That I may cause those who love me to inherit wealth, That I may fill their treasuries.

God wants you to be blessed. God has always wanted you to be blessed.

Proverbs 10:22:

The blessing of the LORD makes one rich, And He adds no sorrow with it.

Psalm 68:19:

Blessed be the Lord, Who daily loads us with benefits, The God of our salvation! Selah

Deuteronomy 28:1-2:

[1] Now it shall come to pass, if you diligently obey the voice of the LORD your God, to observe carefully all His commandments which I command you today, that the LORD your God will set you high above all nations of the earth. [2] And all these blessings shall come upon you and overtake you, because you obey the voice of the LORD your God.

(also read through verse 14).

John 15:7:

If you abide in Me, and My words abide in you, you will ask what you desire, and it shall be done for you.

Deuteronomy 8:18:

And you shall remember the LORD your God, for it is He who gives you power to get wealth, that He may establish His covenant which He swore to your fathers, as it is this day.

Point #7:

Declare aloud your receipt of the thing needed or desired.

Mark 11:23 says:

For assuredly, I say to you, whoever says to this mountain, 'Be removed and be cast into the sea,' and does not doubt in his heart, but believes that those things he says will be done, **he will have whatever he says.** *(Emphasis mine)*

As we went through these scriptures, our spirits were being charged and electrified. Gloria asked David, "Do you see the light in the Word of God?"

David overwhelmingly said he did.

Gloria explained that the supplications were designed to do that when they are backed by scripture. They are designed to bring life—the life of the Father, the provision—the provision of the Father.

Supplications are not designed to be just words. They are designed to be a life-giving source. Do you recall the scripture that says, "...and the Word became flesh." The Word is designed to bring forth whatever its purpose is. The Word for you may become healing. It may become provision. It may become a strength. The Word became....

The *zoe* life of Christ is in the Word. That is what the angels act upon as you commission and co-labor with them. This is what they act upon. This is what you commission them to do. They look forward to receiving this from you to execute their task and their assignment in your life.

Now, do you better understand Isaiah 55:11.

[11] ...so shall My word be that goes forth from My mouth; it shall not return to Me void, but it shall accomplish what I please, and it shall prosper in the thing for which I sent it.

It cannot come back to Him without having fulfilled its purpose. Has no choice but to accomplish what he sent it for. That is its assignment. If you put a post in the ground, things planted are designed to grow and it will try to root in the ground. That is why, after a few years, you must replace the post because it has rotted out at the bottom. It has tried to grow ever since it was planted. The soil is designed to grow anything placed in it. If you place a penny in the ground, after a while, you can see that the soil has tried to cause that penny to grow. That is the nature of soil.

Its assignment is to grow and multiply. Our assignment is to do the same thing based on Genesis 1:28.

A flood of scriptures was coming to mind at this point...more than we could record.

———·———

Chapter 14
Naming the Requisition

As part of this process, the requisition must be named. What is assigned to the items on the requisition? What is it sent to do? It is like a mailing address. *My word goes forth*—it goes out, but what does it go out to do? Where is it designed to land?

For example, in Acts 1, the disciples and the women with Mary were in prayer and supplication in one accord for several days after Jesus' ascension but before the answer was delivered on the day of Pentecost. The landing place for that prayer and supplication was the upper room on the Day of Pentecost.

For Daniel, it was for the children of Israel's freedom from Babylonian captivity. It was the same principle but a different purpose. **Just like a curse must have a place to land, so a blessing or the requisition must have a place to land.**

The last part of Isaiah 55:11 says, "...it shall prosper in the thing for which I sent it." That is the place where it must land. That is the destination. That word is also used for appointment, or to sow it or to shoot it forth.

The requisition, which includes the supplication with the scripture(s), is the sign of the approval because it sets the precedent. Somebody must approve business requisitions.

A petition plus the precedent equals a supplication, resulting in a requisition, resulting in acquisition.

Many simply considered a petition and a supplication to be the same thing. The Father wanted to approve it, but the legal precedent was not set. There were things missing. The petition was waiting on some things as if it were asking, "Can I do this for David? What scripture does he have that I can attach to this petition?" **The provision is already in inventory. It was already built, assembled, packaged, and waiting for someone to pick it up and put it into the delivery system.**

It is already in Heaven's warehouse. We often talk about how Heaven said 2024 is fully funded, meaning that which has already been designed for LifeSpring, Heaven Down Business, or Sandhills Ecclesia—it is already fully funded. Still, we needed supplications with scripture to obtain the requisition for the acquisition of it.

Different from the manufacturing style of the last several years of just-in-time inventory, Heaven has not operated by just-in-time even. Nothing is *ever* on backorder.

Understanding Heaven's Requisition System

In some cases, when I go to the Finance Department for the ministry, I will sign a requisition that George will have prepared for me. However, in the Court of Supplications & Acquisitions, once the court requirements are fulfilled, I do not have to sign off on the requisition. That is already done automatically by the blood of Jesus. It is an automatic process.

David received an image that described the process. He got an image of a petition without a scripture. Once the supplications are created (by linking a petition to a scripture that creates the precedent, they go into a queue to be executed or sent out.

The petitions that are on the records without the scripture have already been put in place to be released. Once the precedent based on the scripture is assigned to it, it goes in the queue for delivery.

Isaiah 55:11 says:

11 ...so shall My word be that goes forth from My mouth....

Assigning the Word to the supplication releases the activation of it. That action creates the next step. For example, I make a petition for resources for my family, I add Philippians 4:19 and 2 Peter 3:1 to it, then I present these to the magistrate in the Court of Supplications and I say with the words of my mouth, "Father, I thank you for the fulfillment of this supplication on my behalf because of my sonship." That activates the requisition.

Confession with the Mouth

A confession with the mouth is also attached to this process; however, the blood of Jesus has already signed it.

In previous years, the Word of Faith movement was strong on confession, but they were not strong on hearing and working from the spirit. They were often working from the soul. The benefit for the Word of Faith people was that they knew to attach the word to some things, but because they were still doing it from their soul, it restricted the benefits coming to them. This requires a transition from soul to spirit in the process of receiving provision or whatever else is needed.

"...so shall my word be that goes out of my mouth. It will not return void..."

When we agree and we attach the Word of God to the supplication—God's spoken word, it becomes alive.

Deuteronomy 30:14 says,

...but the word is very near you, in your mouth and in your heart that you may do it.

Now, that is quoted also in Romans 10:8:

The word is near you, in your mouth and in your heart. That is the word of faith, which we preach.

In John 6:33, Jesus said, "My word is spirit, and my word is life."

As we make the complete supplication with the scriptures, and then we thank him for the manifestation of it, why would there be a need for us to sign off on it? Jesus has already signed off on it. We have met the approval process. That step of the process is automatically handled for us.

Chapter 15

Acquisitions

That brings us to the other part of this court, the acquisitions aspect that we receive by faith. I must see it done, even though I may not see it with my physical eyes. I see it in the eyes of my spirit, not unlike a pregnant woman. She may not see that baby, but she knows she is pregnant. Nobody around her may not see it, but she knows nobody is convincing her otherwise. Eventually, EVERYONE will see it.

There is a seed, a time, and a harvest.

Because acquisition in this definition is "the process of obtaining something or a thing that is obtained past tense." It is already obtained. Now, we will acquire.

It is like 1 Peter 2:24 compared to Isaiah 53: Isaiah looked forward to the cross, but Peter looked back to the cross because it was already done.

These things are in our rearview mirror, and the little imprint on the mirror says, "Objects in the mirror closer than they appear." With what we are talking about right now, the objects in the mirror (the provision that was purchased for us at Calvary and the resurrection), are closer than they would appear to our eyes.

Because we are already seated in Him, **we are already there**. We just have not functioned as if we were.

One of the principles of quantum physics is the duality principle. You are both here *and* there at the same time. But, in addition, we are not only here and seated in heavenly places, we are in our future, and we can also be in our past just as easily as we are in our future.

David's Acquisition

David shared an experience of this concerning his late wife, Regina:

> *Once Regina passed away, one day I thought, 'Lord, you knew this day was going to be here before I was ever created, so I lift my hands and I ask you to give me the download for this moment forward.'*
>
> *I just believed once I went through the grief process. I was not sure how to navigate from that point on. We are talking about living 30+ years with the same person every day. I believed whatever I was needed from that point forward was already given to me when I asked him for it now, and he did everything right here in front of me. Consciously, it was not, but I believed I received*

it. That was an acquisition. That download was the acquisition of my prior supplication.

. . . .

We inquired of Malcolm, asking, "Can you tell us more about acquisitions?"

"An acquisition is when you have requested something, and you obtain it. You are acquiring something."

Malcolm asked Stephanie (referring to the engagement discussed in Chapter 19 on *Becoming a Friend*), "Stephanie, what did you acquire today?"

Stephanie responded, "That it is finished."

Inquiring of Malcolm, I asked, "Through this process, in the end, we receive from Heaven, and we acquire a friend-to-friend relationship?"

Stephanie remarked, "The first question that went through my head was, 'Can you step out of this relational thing?'"

Malcolm asked, "Why would you?"

Stephanie responded, "I know, I know. I get that, but you can step out of it if you choose to."

Malcolm replied, "Free will is free will, just choose you on this day whom you will serve. You have a choice in intimacy. But why would you leave?"

Stephanie answered, "I know, I do not want to leave this place.

> *"It is the end desire of Heaven that every son becomes a friend."*

Malcolm added,

> *"The end goal of the Kingdom is for every son to come to this place."*

Stephanie remarked, "I just got a picture of this court from a bird's eye view. I see, we are in the chamber of the Father's heart. It became small, this courtroom, but I see it located in His heart. Wow!"

———·———

Chapter 16

What are you saying?

What are you saying? Scripture says in Mark 11:24:

Believe that you receive it, and you should have what you say....

Mark 11:23-24:

²³ For assuredly, I say to you, whoever says to this mountain, 'Be removed and be cast into the sea,' and does not doubt in his heart, but believes that those things he says will be done, he will have whatever he says. ²⁴ Therefore I say to you, whatever things you ask when you pray, believe that you receive them, and you will have them.

Confession activates the requisition.

Our confession should be our spirit speaking through our body and our soul, not resisting that process. The spirit already knows what is in the mind of the Father. Our spirit already knows the heart of the Father on every matter. As we speak, as our spirit speaks, our soul is to be a conduit.

I am aware that there is now a requisition in place, but the movement to acquire it or the acquisition of it was still hanging in the balance. Once I spoke it and I released it, it became life. It became reality.

I took what was invisible and brought it into the visible world as such. We need to ask ourselves, "Is what we are saying words of faith?" Faith is all the evidence you need of the things not seen. It becomes the substance of things.

Hebrews 11:1 in the Amplified Translation gives an additional perspective:

> *Now, faith is the assurance, the confirmation, the title deed of the things we hope for being the proof, the things we do not see, and conviction of their reality. Faith perceiving as real fact what is not revealed to the senses. (AMP)*

---
*Faith divinely guarantees
the evidence of things not seen.*

It is the conviction of their reality. Faith comprehends as fact what cannot be experienced by the physical senses.

> *Persuasion confirms confident expectation and proves the unseen world to be more real than the seen. Faith celebrates as certain what hope visualizes as future. (The shadow no longer substitutes the substance. Jesus is the substance of things hoped for, the evidence of everything the*

prophets foretold. The unveiling of Christ in human life completes mankind's every expectation). (MIRROR)

Verse three says,

³ Faith alone can explain what is not apparent to the natural eye; how the ages were perfectly framed by the Word of God. Now we understand that everything visible has its origin in the invisible.

⁵ Enoch enjoyed God's favor by faith. In spite of Adam's fall, he proved that faith defeats death. (His absent body prophesied the resurrection of Christ; faith does not die).

⁶ There's no substitute reward for faith. Faith's return exceeds any other sense of achievement. Faith knows that God is those who desire to respond to his invitation, to draw near realize by faith that he is life's most perfect gift.

⁷ Noah received Divine instruction to save his household from judgment; faith prompted him to construct the Ark immediately, long before the rains were evident. His faith demonstrated the difference between judgment and justification.

For the Hebrews 11 saints, it was as good as done the moment they said it was.

The acquisition means that we have already acquired it. It is already finished. Look at the process. Look at the steps from beginning to end,

Petition plus scripture equals supplication, resulting in a requisition that ends up as acquisition. That becomes the basis for acquisition. And when you acquire something, you have received the thing that you have asked.

As you receive it by faith, you thank him for taking care of it, that it has already been done because, in Heaven, it has already been done. One definition of acquisition says an asset or object bought, obtained, or purchased.[15]

What we acquire becomes an asset to us.

It may be something you get a title deed for. We must also exercise stewardship toward the thing(s) we acquire.

If I am extending faith for a new vehicle, I know that Heaven pays attention to how I honor the vehicle I am currently using. I am sure you have seen vehicles that were piled high with trash, cups, food wrappers, etc. They do not exhibit an atmosphere where the Glory of God would be present. I have found that the Glory likes an uncluttered environment. My stewardship of one thing dictates the reception of the next thing. Take responsibility for what you have obtained and honor the Lord with it. It is simply the way promotion works. How I take care of what I have qualifies me for advancement to

---

[15]Oxford Dictionary. https://www.google.com/search?client=firefox-b-1-d&q=acquisition

the next better thing. Let us steward well the natural *AND* the supernatural.

———·———

Chapter 17
A Daily Routine?

All petitions should be borne out of intimacy. We see in the book of Daniel where he was known to make petitions three times a day (Daniel 6:13). Even in spite of tremendous opposition, Daniel would not be moved. It went so far as the king having him put in the lion's den, but the Lord kept him safe, to the astonishment of the king.

King David discovered the results of intimacy with the Father and described it in Psalm 37:4-7:

> *4 Delight yourself also in the LORD, and He shall give you the desires of your heart.*
>
> *5 Commit your way to the LORD, trust also in Him, and He shall bring it to pass.*
>
> *6 He shall bring forth your righteousness as the light, and your justice as the noonday.*
>
> *7 Rest in the LORD and wait patiently for Him; do not fret because of him who prospers in his way,*

because of the man who brings wicked schemes to pass.

It is the desire of the Father to give you the desires of your heart. However, in a self-consuming culture, we often find ourselves being selfish in our petitions.

James 4:3 tells us a reason we do not receive answers is because we want something for the wrong reason(s). Your six-year-old may want a Lamborghini for Christmas, but it is not wisdom to fulfill that request.

Deuteronomy 8:18 says:

And you shall remember the LORD your God, for it is He who gives you power to get wealth, that He may establish His covenant which He swore to your fathers, as it is this day.

The purpose of the wealth is to establish God's covenant in the earth. That should be our focus for whatever we receive from Heaven. It is not that the Father does not want us to have good things, but what is our "why" for those things? Will it puff us up? Will it give us bragging rights on some level? Or will it *truly* bring the Father glory?

Daniel was a devout man who made it a point in His life to make supplications three times a day. That was his determination. I suggest you follow Heaven's instructions in how often you should do this. I would recommend that you access the Court of Supplications and Acquisitions often as you are ingesting this revelation to make sure you do not have petitions on appeal or with liens upon them.

You want to clean up any deficits of scripture on your petitions, so they qualify as supplications.

It may be helpful to have someone assist you as you step into Heaven to check the status of your petitions and supplications. With the information you have gleaned thus far, you have no good reason not to have your petitions fully in order. The process is simple, and the resources are available for you now. Let us not wait another day!

Keep a Log

Another simple practice is to keep a log of supplications and their acquisition. It will be a good source of encouragement in your life as you recount the blessings of the Lord and the expressions of His goodness toward you.

It does not have to be highly involved. Simply ask Heaven to show you the best way for you to do it. Think of all the black eyes your enemy will be receiving as Heaven shows up on your behalf time after time.

———·———

Chapter 18
Greater Measure

As Stephanie and I engaged Heaven, we were inquiring about more information about the Court of Supplications and Acquisitions. We wanted to know what the heart of the Father was concerning it. We were grateful and thankful for the opportunity to come into such a magnificent place through Jesus.

Stephanie found herself standing at the door, and Jesus kissed her on the cheek and let me in. The court seemed empty. A woman in white was in the room, and she offered Stephanie a seat at a wooden desk. Stephanie sat down, and the woman placed a notebook in front of her so that she could take notes.

She did not see the magistrate (whom we had seen before), but we did see an American flag (for some reason). She asked what she was supposed to do, and as she did, a movie started to play. It reminded Stephanie of the old newsreels they would play at the beginning of movies during World War II. She saw what was a depiction of the beginning before time when the Lord was creating these courts.

She said, "I am seeing the foundations of Heaven. I see The Spirit of Wisdom being a part of all of this. I see the instructions to the angels to build out these courts."

In the middle of the film, Wisdom turned to her and said, "We knew you would be here. These were constructed because we knew you would be here. We knew you would come in obedience."

Stephanie remarked to me, "I have a knowing that Heaven meant the saints that were willing to come. We still have a choice."

Wisdom (still talking to Stephanie in the motion picture) said, "These courts were designed because of the willful subjugation and obedience to the heart of the Father by the saints."[16]

Stephanie asked, "What is it we are supposed to take note of? I am grateful that before the foundations of the world, you created these things for us for such a time as this."

The woman then began to teach us. She began speaking about this court—the Court of Supplications and Acquisitions and said, "The *willful act* of the saints **laid the foundation** for these courts. This is why it takes

---

[16] Subjugation: The action of bringing someone or something under domination or control. (Oxford Dictionary)

relationship in this courtroom. Even though there is a magistrate, this place comes from the highest courts.

---

*"Relationship is the
only way of access in this court."*

Wisdom said, "Deep intimacy brings a greater measure in this place."

Stephanie noted that 'measure' was a key word here. As we watched, the magistrate, who was seated at his bench, looked over a court case in front of him. He never looked up but rather, looked through the case, then with a pound from his gavel, moved to the next case.

The woman said, "Greater measure."

Stephanie asked her what that meant in this court.

The woman asked, "What is the height and the depth and the breadth of Him?"

Stephanie replied, "What is it that you want us to learn? What do we need to know to do here?"

The magistrate has looked up now and said, "Know that this is where the answers come from."

Stephanie then noticed a scale on his desk and asked, "Why is there a scale?"

The magistrate said, "There is a tipping point."

Stephanie asked, "Magistrate, is this like when we have our prayers that fill the bowl, and there's a tipping point?"

The magistrate replied, "There's greater measure here."

I suggested to Stephanie, "Ask him what question we should ask him."

Stephanie inquired, "What question should we ask?"

The magistrate said, "What is the tipping point?"

Stephanie asked, "What *is* the tipping point?"

He replied, "Love."

Slightly confused, Stephanie said, "I need help understanding because I understand love. I understand that love is why we are here."

The magistrate stopped her, putting his hand up, and said, "You're here because of intimacy."

Stephanie asked, "But isn't that love?"

He replied, "Once you've reached this place, you have reached the tipping point."

Stephanie queried, "You mean this court, magistrate?"

The magistrate asked, "What measure is offered here?"

Stephanie asked him, "Is that the question I should ask?"

He had Stephanie stand up and asked her, "Who are you?"

She replied, "I am a son."

He remarked, "That is the measuring point. You are at the tipping point. You have a say here."

Stephanie questioned, "Are you saying that, in this court, I can speak and make a statement as a supplication? Yet, magistrate, it would feel more like a decree to me. However, I think you are saying I can state, as a supplication—as a son, in this court with the measuring scales leaning on my behalf, that the tipping point has been met for these supplications and prayers to be answered?"

He replied, "You've got the idea. Keep going."

Stephanie paused to ask me what I thought about what was just said.

I replied, "Well, like it says, in 1st John 3:21-22, that if we know that He hears us, we know we have the petitions we have desired of Him. The fact that He hears us *is the granting of the supplication*. We are simply coming to agreement with the fact that He hears us out of our intimacy with Him."

Intimacy Produces Results

The magistrate said, "Intimacy is not conditional. Intimacy is intimacy."

"It is a desire of His heart, *and* it is *our desire matching His desire*."

> *"Intimacy is our desire matching His desire."*

I asked him, "Is this where we are making the transition from the son-to-Father style of prayer to the friend-to-friend style?"

The magistrate stood up, and he clapped his hands.

I remarked, "A friend just tells you what's on their heart, and because they trusted you as their friend, the answers come even if it was inconvenient for the one they were asking of."

The magistrate handed the gavel to Jesus and stepped out of the way, The gavel then came down, and we were immediately moved out of the court we had been in.

Stephanie found herself standing on a mountaintop. There was wind around her, and it was like she was seeing the clouds, and she watched the wind form into little bits and pieces of her life across the sky. It was simply an outline of her doing life, and Jesus was standing beside her.

Jesus said to her. "All of those moments led you to here."

Jesus pointed out that a distinction exists between the son praying to the Father style of prayer and the friend-to-friend paradigm of prayer. In the son to Father prayer, they will ask and keep on asking. However, with the friend-to-friend prayer, the friend only needs to be asked once.

Jesus then took Stephanie by the hand and said, "You are my friend. It is finished."

Stephanie replied, "Thank you, Jesus."

The Mountain of the Lord

Jesus then said, "You're on the mountain of the Lord."

Stephanie remarked, "There is so much wind, but it is not like the kind of wind that would blow you down. It is just going through me and around me."

Suddenly she was back in the courtroom, but it was empty, and the magistrate was gone, but the lady was still present.

The woman said, "He (Jesus) said, 'It is finished.'"

Stephanie remarked, "He said that on the cross."

The woman noted, "He said it today."

Stephanie replied, "I know that today means much more than just today, but what do we do?"

The woman took her by the hand and said, "Come back any time."

Puzzled, Stephanie said, "I don't know exactly what just happened."

The woman said, "All you have to know is that it is finished."

Stephanie said, "It makes me just want to sit down and not ever leave this place."

The woman said, "Yeah, this court has that effect on people. Abraham and David were here."

I noted, "It has more of the feel of a cozy living room than a court."

We inquired of the woman for her name, but she was not forthcoming with that information. She simply patted Stephanie on the hand and then placed her hand on Stephanie's chest.

The woman said, "I bless her soul to understand."

Stephanie said, "I would like for the Spirit of Understanding to help me through this process."

I added, "Me too!"

Stephanie closed by saying, "Thank you. I know that the Lord's heart would never want people to feel like they are not accepted, but in any relationship, you must be in a relationship, to be in a different place with people. What is interesting is that they set it up before the foundations of the world, knowing that we would come. There is something to this because we do have a choice not to come."

Our engagement with the woman in the courtroom ended, but more was to be shared another time.

——— · ———

Chapter 19
Becoming a Friend

In Matthew 7, Jesus taught his disciples about two forms of prayer: The 'son praying to the Father', and the 'friend-to-friend' paradigm of prayer. What the Father is wanting us to gain from this understanding of the Court of Supplications and Acquisitions is that we progress from 'son-to-Father' praying to praying out of friendship.

Abraham was known as a friend of God, as James stated in James 2:33:

And the Scripture was fulfilled which says, 'ABRAHAM BELIEVED GOD, AND IT WAS ACCOUNTED TO HIM FOR RIGHTEOUSNESS.' And he was called the friend of God.

Abraham had developed such a relationship with the Father that God was fond of him.

Aspects of Friendship

Aspects of friendship are:

- You share secrets.
- You can depend upon them in a pinch.
- Your friends will come to your aid.
- They will stick up for you.
- They will believe in you when others may not.

Consider these characteristics in light of Jesus and the Father being your friend. How would things be different for you? In John 15, Jesus was meeting with his disciples and shared how they could be considered His friends:

John 15:14-17:

14 You are My friends if you do whatever I command you.

15 No longer do I call you servants, for a servant does not know what his master is doing; but I have called you friends, for all things that I heard from My Father I have made known to you.

16 You did not choose Me, but I chose you and appointed you that you should go and bear fruit, and that your fruit should remain, that whatever you ask the Father in My name He may give you.

17 These things I command you, that you love one another. (Emphasis added)

Things have not changed. His command is to love one another...that is the pathway to friendship with Jesus.

We have examples of persons in Scripture who were known as a "friend of God." Abraham is one of the first who had that designation, as we saw previously in James 2:23.

Moses also shared this designation as we see in Exodus 33:11:

So the LORD spoke to Moses face to face, as a man speaks to his friend. And he (Moses) would return to the camp, but his servant Joshua the son of Nun, a young man, did not depart from the tabernacle.

In this passage we see that Joshua, Moses successor was building a life of intimacy with the Father as Moses had. Joshua did not depart from the tabernacle, but remained in the presence of Yahweh. Friendship has to be pursued.

As King David was known as a man after God's own heart, I think we can safely say he was a friend of God as well.

Many others would qualify as friends of God throughout scripture. Will you be one added to the list?

——— · ———

Chapter 20

Epilogue

As David and I stepped into the Library of Revelation for further information about this book, Jonathan, whom we had met before, came to instruct us. The information flowed from Jonathan to David like a river. Here is what Jonathan had to say:

> *This revelation has created a new 'landing pad', a new place to operate from, that positions you into greater authority because of the information you are now privy to. With this place comes greater responsibility, not just a greater awareness.*
>
> *This information is not for the faint; it is not for the weak. It is for those who are ready to embrace their sonship in all the maturity that goes with it. For many, it is going to cause accelerated growth where they would have to mature fast. Many who will come into this revelation have been hesitant. This revelation is a launching force. The shooting of this arrow—the new landing pad, will cause you*

to hit the bullseye as you execute the legal court work.

This is not just about getting prayers answered, but this is governing from a different place. It is governing as the Father would have you to govern. For many, it takes years for them to get to this place, like unto maturing in certain areas of your life, it takes years. Yet the Father has ordained and assigned you, Ron, to be like Moses, leading the people out. You understand authority. You understand governance, and so must the people understand authority and governance.

When the Word of God says that where you put your feet, you shall possess the land, these are not mere words that you already know, but for many, these words have become cliches, and that is not the intent of Heaven. The intent is for the sons to rule, to reign, and to govern their territories. This is also what is meant that the Kingdom of God comes in Earth as it is in Heaven. I am familiar with kingdom order. My father was a king, and this new landing pad is a place of kingdom order. Kingdom order will be the strategy, the plan, and the norm.

This landing pad is equipped with the oil of ease. It is not to be a place of struggle. It is to be a place of being, abiding in sonship, and operating as governors. Remember, in this Court of Supplications, Satan has no entrance. He is not allowed. This place, this landing pad, is designed that the Word of God would be executed and carried out, but it is a co-laboring with the sons of God and with Heaven.

Those who operate in this court must see themselves as God sees them. You must see yourselves as the eyes, the ears, the hands, the feet, the voice, the heart, the body of Christ. Heaven is excited.

We are exuberant; we are ecstatic. The angels, the myriad of angels are excited because now this is a different type of commissioning. Whereas before, you had to verbally commission the angels. But when you apply the Word of God to your supplications, there is an automatic release and enforcing and carrying out of that word and the answer to the supplications.[17]

As you embark on this journey—this new adventure, like you have embraced previous revelations, embrace this revelation. Embrace this opportunity, this new access to greater revelation and to the unfolding of the heart of God for his people. Embrace it with all your faith, and remember, operate from a place of love, the love of the Father.

Remember, the Word says that He is touched with the feeling of your infirmities.[18] *For many have*

---

[17] Psalm 103:20, Bless the LORD, you His angels, Who excel in strength, who do His word, Heeding the voice of His word.

[18] Hebrews 4:15, For we do not have a High Priest who cannot sympathize with our weaknesses, but was in all *points* tempted as *we are, yet* without sin.

dealt with issue after issue after issue. It was like an infirmity because it was so constant. But you have been given a weapon, a resource, and authority. It is also an answering of the call to operate from your mountain simultaneously.

Let me add that. Do you see where the revelations have built upon each other over the last year? Your books have built on each other. You have caused the character of Christ to be developed in those who will receive and embrace the revelations. Enjoy! And Ron, as you always say, have fun!

———·———

Appendix

Resources for Scripture Research

Numerous resources exist to help you in finding scriptures that help establish the legal precedent needed for supplications.

I work a great deal from my laptop and use an online Bible software known as e-Sword (e-sword.net). The developer of this software has made the basic version available for free on the Internet. It comes with a few basic translations, and many other translations can be added by purchasing the license for them. He does not charge for the basic software, but I encourage you to donate to him for his product. It enables him to develop it further.

Online sources include Bible.com (YouVersion), BibleGateway.com, and BlueLetterBible.org, just to name a few. Online searches will reveal lists of scriptures on a variety of topics. For example, concerning healing, conduct a search for Healing Scriptures, and you will have plenty of options. Make this more than an academic exercise, though. Pay attention to Holy Spirit, your angels, men, or women in white who can assist you and point you to appropriate passages.

To build your faith, pray in the spirit, and while you do, read Hebrews 11, where we read of the exploits of many men and women who saw God show up in their situations. Remember, what He did for one, He will do for another. Because we have these examples in scripture it can encourage us to extend our faith for the granting of the supplications we have made before the Lord.

———·———

Resources from LifeSpring International Ministries

A visit to the **RonHorner.com** website will give a glimpse of the various branches of ministry we are involved in. We started out providing coaching to people within the Courts of Heaven advocating for them and their situations. Our corporate name is LifeSpring International Ministries, Inc., a North Carolina registered nonprofit.

Personal Advocacy Sessions

Known as Personal Advocacy Sessions, these 90-minute sessions with our trained team of advocates have successfully worked with a myriad of situations.

LifeSpring Mentoring Group

Since starting this weekly class on Zoom in 2019, we have taught on the Courts of Heaven, protocols, engaging Heaven for revelation, working with angels and men and women white linen, lingering human spirits, and more. It is a free class. Simply visit **ronhorner.com** to register for the link for the class.

Membership Program

We have several tiers of membership for those tracking with us. The Platinum level gains you access to our library of videos, blogs, and more. Again, visit the website.

CourtsNet

CourtsNet is our video-based training program offering a wide variety of classes and courses. We also have our Facilitator Training Program, an 11-month school to learn more about the Courts of Heaven, its protocols and how to serve as an advocate in the Courts of Heaven. We have a weekly live class on Mondays and also have a solo option for those unable to commit to the Monday schedule. We also have a school in Switzerland and are planning to open one in South Africa in 2024. Visit CourtsNet.com.

AfterCare

Not every situation is solved by the Courts of Heaven. Sometimes people need to learn simple things to navigate life. Our AfterCare program provides Biblical counseling, classes, and groups regularly.

Sandhills Ecclesia

In 2022, we started a Sunday Gathering known as Sandhills Ecclesia (that's the name we saw on the book in Heaven when we went to inquire.) My wife, Adina, and I live in the area of North Carolina known as the Sandhills region, thus the name. We meet weekly at 11:00 AM Eastern, and on the first Sunday of the month, we have an afternoon gathering to do legislative work in the Courts of Heaven as a group. All are welcome. Simply visit **sandhillsecclesia.com** and register for the link.

Heaven Down Business

Heaven Down Business is a worldwide coaching and consultancy business designed to assist entrepreneurs and business owners in implementing the Heaven Down™ Business Building paradigm into their business. For more information, visit heavendownbusiness.com.

Adina's Melodies/Heaven Down Music

Adina Horner, co-founder, is a gifted minstrel and has several albums of prophetic worship music available on several of the most popular music platforms. Visit **adinasmelodies.com**.

LifeSpring Publishing/Scroll Publishers

LifeSpring Publishing primarily publishes Dr. Ron's books, and Scroll Publishers is our imprint where we publish the books of others relating to engaging Heaven, living spirit forward and the Heaven Down™ lifestyle.

YouTube Channel

Our most recent videos from the Mentoring Group are posted on YouTube®. Visit our YouTube® channel, **courtsofheavenwebinar** on YouTube® for the latest videos.

RonHorner.com

Our website, **RonHorner.com,** has a myriad of resources, many of which are free, as well as numerous videos.

Description

Do you have prayers for which you are still seeking answers? Learn how to turn your petition into a supplication in order to have the answers come. Discover some of the reasons our prayers have been "on appeal" by the enemy and learn how to get these appeals removed.

Intimacy is the basis of operations in the Court of Supplications and Acquisitions and to be a friend of God is crucial. Learn how to discover a life built on friendship with the Father and how to operate from your personal Mountain of the Lord.

———·———

About the Author

Dr. Ron Horner is an apostolic teacher specializing in the Courts of Heaven. He has written over thirty books on the Courts of Heaven, engaging Heaven, working with angels, or living from revelation.

He currently trains people in engaging the Courts of Heaven in a weekly online teaching session. You can register to participate and discover more about the Courts of Heaven prayer paradigm on his various websites, classes, products, and services found here:

www.ronhorner.com

Other Books by Dr. Ron M. Horner

Building Your Business from Heaven Down

Building Your Business from Heaven Down 2.0

Building Your Business with the Blueprint of Heaven

Commissioning Angels – Volume 1

Cooperating with The Glory

Courts of Heaven Process Charts

Dealing with Trusts & Consequential Liens

Engaging Angels in the Realms of Heaven

Engaging Heaven for Revelation – Volume 1

Engaging Heaven for Revelation – Volume 2

Engaging Heaven for Trade

Engaging the Courts for Ownership & Order

Engaging the Courts for Your City (*Paperback, Leader's Guide & Workbook*)

Engaging the Courts of Healing & the Healing Garden

Engaging the Courts of Heaven

Engaging the Help Desk of the Courts of Heaven

Four Keys to Dismantling Accusations

Freedom from Mithraism

Kingdom Dynamics – Volume 1

Kingdom Dynamics – Volume 2

Let's Get it Right!

Lingering Human Spirits

Lingering Human Spirits – Volume 2

Living Spirit Forward

Next Dimension Access to the Court of Supplications

Overcoming the False Verdicts of Freemasonry

Overcoming Verdicts from the Courts of Hell

Releasing Bonds from the Courts of Heaven

The Courts of Heaven: An Introduction
(formerly *Engaging the Mercy Court of Heaven*)

Unlocking Spiritual Seeing

Working with Your Realms and Your Realm Angels

SPANISH

Cómo Anular los Falsos Veredictos de la Masonería

Cómo Proceder en la Corte Celestial de Misericordia

Cómo Proceder en las Cortes para su Ciudad

Cómo Trabajar con Angeles en los Ambitos del Cielo

Cooperando con La Gloria de Dios

Las Cuatro Llaves para Anular las Acusaciones

Liberando Bonos en las Cortes Celestiales

Liberando Su Visión Espiritual

Sea Libre del Mitraísmo

Tablas de Proceso de la Cortes del Cielo

———·———

Notes

Notes

www.ingramcontent.com/pod-product-compliance
Lightning Source LLC
Chambersburg PA
CBHW031628160426
43196CB00006B/329